BEGGING
FOR
CHANGE

HarperBusiness
An Imprint of HarperCollins*Publishers*

BEGGING
CHANGE

FOR

THE DOLLARS
AND SENSE
OF MAKING
NONPROFITS
RESPONSIVE,
EFFICIENT, AND
REWARDING
FOR ALL

ROBERT EGGER

with Howard Yoon

Permission to reprint 2002 Donor and Recipient Charts from the AAFRC kindly granted by the AAFRC.

"Highlights of the 2002 GuideStar Nonprofit Compensation Report" courtesy of Guidestar Philanthropic Research Inc. © 2002, Philanthropic Research, Inc. (GuideStar), Williamsburg, Va. Reprinted with permission.

Permission to reprint "Giving and Volunteering Key Findings" kindly granted by the Independent Sector.

HarperCollins books may be purchased for educational, business, or sales promotional use. For information, please write to: Special Markets Department, HarperCollins Publishers Inc., 10 East 53rd Street, New York, New York 10022.

Designed by William Ruoto

Library of Congress Cataloging-In-Publication Data

Egger, Robert.
    Begging for change : the dollars and sense of making nonprofits responsive, efficient, and rewarding for all
        p.   cm.
    Includes index.
    ISBN 0-06-054171-7
    1. Charities—Management.   2. Charities—Finance.
3. Nonprofit organizations—Management.   4. Nonprofit organizations—Finance.   5. Poor—Services for—United States.
6. Egger, Robert.   7. DC Central Kitchen—Case studies.
I. Yoon, Howard.   II. Title.

HV41.E35   2004
361.7'068—dc22   2003057094

04   05   06   07   08   /   10   9   8   7   6   5   4   3   2   1

To Claudia and Julia—I fight for you
And to Joe Strummer and Joey Ramone

ACKNOWLEDGMENTS

There have been hundreds, if not thousands, who have contributed an ear, and arm, their time and their brains to making Kitchen what it is. I am indebted to you all. The following is a weak attempt to remember those whose actions and commitment demand acknowledgment. I ask the forgiveness of anyone I thoughtlessly omitted.

To the Friends of My Young Heart: Donna Zick, Janice Reece, Jane Humpstone, Christina Martin, Heather Parsons, Lisa DeYoung, Katherine Kagel, Rob Johnson, "Uncle" Dick, Bill Bolling, Mike Mulqueen, Steve Farr, Julia Erikson, Linda Volger, Jill Bullard, and everyone who helped build Foodchain. We was good.

Foundation Friends (the ones with eyes): The Abel Foundation (for taking it out of my head), the W.H. Donner Foundation (for taking it national), and the folks at PM; Richard Brown, Sandra Blau, Karen Brosius, Jennifer Goodale, Jane Tally, John Barnes and Shawna Aarons (for funding Community Kitchens when nobody else would), and Steve Brady at Sodexho for letting us team with your team to make Campus Kitchens happen. And a special thanks to Clem Hannrahan and Gary Lee at the UPS Foundation for being humble, generous, and for being there at Foodchain at the very beginning.

For Friends in the Field (who think big): Visionary Bill Ayers and WHY, Big-Hearted Glen Howard, Super Mensch Rob Fersch, Professors Ann Hale and Teresa O'Conner, Ellen Teller, my friends at FRAC, and the amazing students at the Cornell University School of Hotel Administration, Honest John Morrill and Handsome Ed Cooney and each of the fantastic Congressional Hunger Fellows, Rep. Tony Hall and his trusty sidekick Max Finberg, USDA partners Dan Glickman, Shirley Watkins, Eric Bost and the infamous Joel Berg, The Marriott family, Eric Peterson and the ASFSA Crew, and everyone who thinks beyond territory and turf.

Big Props to each of the DCCK Board Chairs: Rick, Cindy, Bill, Rob, Penny, Rheba, and Jose, as well as everyone who has served, worked, and helped build the Kitchen.

Local D.C. Partners: The generous Shaw, Pittman, both the Restaurant and Hotel Associations of Metropolitan Washington (we owe SO much to you), Nextell, The GRI Chefs, UWNCA, Fannie Mae, Leadership Washington, the *Washington Post*, and the *Washington Business Journal*.

Special Friends, Guides, and Loving Confidants: Mueller, Laura Strickler, Katie Couric, the Inspirational Jennifers, Jodi

Lehr, the Unforgettable Laine Forman, my dear Rev. Steve Klingelhopfer, Lyles Carr, Bob Maddigan, Kojo Nnambdi, Jody Manor, Carol Fennelly, Gail Ross, Jim Ryan, Kathy Kretman, Hollywood Pokey, and the amazing Brands-Debby, Anstice and George.

A Special Thanks to everyone who ever worked, volunteered, or studied at the Kitchen: Brothers Gary, Alex Tate, Chefs Abdul Raheem, Sally Rumsey, Susan Callahan, Susan Waterson and Frank "the Rock" McKinney, Isaac, Katherine Newell Smith, Melvin, Eric, Rob, Willy and all the drivers, Suzanne Hechmer, Petra Silton and Chris Johnson, the Hard-Working Karens, The CKP Crew, Natalie Jayroe at KINC, Francis Reed, The Ebony Roses—Marianne and Tammy, Ron "the Compass" Swanson, The Beautiful Ms. Dot, Dr. Neda Farzan and Scott Weier, Eric Swenson and Rose-Catherine, The One and Only Gertrude Higgenbothem, Craig, John and Cisco who hit the streets every day, and the infamous Fifth St. Shorty.

Special props to Chapman Todd (past) and Cynthia Rowland (present) for making the thing run day in and day out with such passion and commitment.

And a special dose of love to my best friend and colleague, the truly amazing Siobhan Canty at Greater D.C. Cares (which, next to the Kitchen, is the coolest program in D.C.).

CONTENTS

PROLOGUE
Hello, My Name Is Robert, and I'm a
Recovering Hypocrite   xv

INTRODUCTION
"Brother, Can You Spare a Dime?" A Brief History
of the Handout   1

CHAPTER ONE
Soup Kitchen Confidential   25

CHAPTER TWO
Doing Good Versus Doing Right   49

CHAPTER THREE
Feeding the Tapirs   61

CHAPTER FOUR
Starfish and Random Acts   69

CHAPTER FIVE
Whom Are You Serving?   81

CHAPTER SIX
$M=EC^2$ 95

CHAPTER SEVEN
The Tangible Link   109

CHAPTER EIGHT
Taking Troy   121

CHAPTER NINE
Take It to 11   133

CHAPTER TEN
Keeping the Faith   143

CHAPTER ELEVEN
Grab the Future by the Face   155

EPILOGUE
Redemption City   169

ROBERT'S RULES FOR NONPROFITS   177

APPENDIX
Giving and Volunteering Statistics and Resources   185

INDEX   207

He who wants to tear down a house must be prepared to rebuild it.

    —African proverb

Smile, you son of a bitch.

    —Chief Brody, *Jaws*

Hello, My Name Is Robert, and I'm a Recovering Hypocrite

D.C. Central is what most people call a "soup kitchen," but I despise that term because it's also a job-training program, a for-profit catering company, a cooking school, a drug-counseling program, a support group, a job bank, a food service institution, an empowerment zone, and a true "model" program. It's a take-no-prisoners, make-no-excuses, well-oiled hunger-fighting machine.

Never mind that the Kitchen cranks out 4,000 meals a day, seven days a week, 365 days a year by collecting and reusing the unserved food that society throws away. Forget the fact that we've designed a 12-week culinary course that trains people who are viewed as society's worst problems—the homeless, the drug addicts, the ex-cons (in other words, people our society throws away)—and turns them into part of the solution.

D.C. Central Kitchen has been a model for more than 50 "community kitchens" around the country. We were named one of President Bush Sr.'s "Thousand Points of Light." We've been featured on *Nightline, 48 Hours,* and the *Today* show as well as in the *New York Times,* the London *Financial Times,* the *Wall Street Journal,* the *Washington Post,* and many other news and print media outlets. Bill and Hillary came to the Kitchen and helped prepare meals. So have Jeff and Beau Bridges. Even Oprah likes what we're doing. A few years ago she and Paul Newman, one of her partners in the effort to help good nonprofit models, gave us $100,000 to help branch out. Now we're moving out into the hundreds of idle school cafeterias across America—in universities, high schools, community colleges—to assist communities that are struggling to meet the increasing need to feed seniors, working families, and kids.

I'm damn proud of everything the men and women at the Kitchen have accomplished over the years. But in the end, D.C. Central always is referred to as a "soup kitchen," a depression-era term that evokes a million outdated stereotypes of charity. Words like "soup kitchen" limit the public's perception of what we in the nonprofit sector can accomplish with places like the Kitchen. It also unfairly influences their larger perception of who's hungry, homeless, and struggling to get by in America.

Why do people still use this term? Because it's an image people know, the one they're comfortable with. But it reinforces the notion that charities haven't changed all that much over the last 100 years, except in size. And the most disturbing part of their attitude is that they're right.

The nonprofit sector, a vast category that includes everything from hospitals, colleges, and museums to political groups, churches, and "soup kitchens," has grown into an $800 billion industry—more than the GNP of Australia, Russia, or all Arab nations combined. It represents nearly 10 percent of our nation's economy and employs 11 million people. Yet even with all the dollars invested, all the hours spent, and the studies and research by the best and brightest, we still haven't been able to move beyond the dated terms and practices of 19th-century charity. We're still in a mode of soup kitchens and handouts, even though some of us in the sector work hard every day to shake that image.

In today's competitive fund-raising climate, too many nonprofits are chasing the money, not their mission. They're begging for money when they need to realize what they need to be doing is begging for change.

And in my fight to change the sector, I've been told by direct mail experts, PR gurus, and hundreds of reporters and nonprofits colleagues who've covered the growth that we have two choices: We can either inform the public about the Kitchen or educate them about their stereotypes and attitude, but not both. I've spent every day of the last 15 years at the Kitchen trying to prove them wrong.

Before I entered the nonprofit sector, I was running nightclubs in Washington, D.C., everything from punk halls to upscale jazz clubs. And you know what? I found that running a successful service nonprofit requires a lot of the same work: a modest dose of bullshit, a serious commitment to the bottom line, and a dedication to putting on a good show day in and day out. As an outsider to the sector, I ran into many "lifers"—

nonprofit veterans who were content doing what they'd always been doing instead of shaking up the system. They seemed more interested in maintaining the status quo with their jobs than searching for new ways to improve their community. I set out to show them another way, to demonstrate that you have to tear down walls, break routines, and look for more efficient ways of running service organizations.

Begging for Change will tell you my story, what I've learned as the head of the D.C. Central Kitchen and as the recent interim head of the United Way of D.C., the second largest United Way chapter in the country. I'll mix in stories from my life running nightclubs and describe how these experiences shaped my views on the nonprofit sector. The book will look at the good, the bad, and the stupid of the nonprofit sector. It will take a critical look at how we should change the way we give and change the way we use what we're given.

For too long we've been focusing on the wrong measurements, the wrong language, the wrong attitude for achieving social progress in our country. It's time to throw away terms like "soup kitchen," the "needy," and even "nonprofit" and to introduce new terms and new battle plans. It's time to ask serious questions of the organizations we donate time or money to. What's the plan? Why should I give? How do you use our money and volunteer hours? Are you perpetuating a cycle of need and dependency, or finding ways to liberate the people you serve? What are your goals in five or 10 years? Are they realistic and on target? These are some of the questions every donor, volunteer, employee, board member, and executive director needs to be able to answer. All of us need to be inculcated with these principles so that we see that our actions are contributing to actual change in our society.

Begging for Change won't drown you in statistics to make you feel guilty, sad, or angry. It won't pander to your emotions or play the pity card. It won't be a feel-good celebration of do-gooders and victims. This is not about building cathedrals; this is about smashing stereotypes and challenging once hallowed institutions. This is about killing sacred cows. This is about people climbing down from the cross so we can use the wood.

A good nonprofit experience should be a freeing experience, like a trip to the mountaintop. That's what this book is all about. I'm going to talk to you about work, and the need to shut up, put our heads down, and get to it. I'm going to talk to you about turf, the need to let it go, and the importance of realizing that what matters isn't what you own or what you have or whether you were there first, but what you do with what you have.

And I'm going to tell all of this to you in a style that is brutally honest, at times infuriating or even annoying, but that always genuinely reflects my journey to find real change and real results in the nonprofit sector. Either I've lost you already with my ranting, or I hope to have you nodding with me before I'm done.

You should think of this book as two things: a guide to giving and a guide to doing. It's a weapon in your fight against stereotypes, complacency, and narrow thinking. It's a meditation on what we haven't achieved in the 100 years of nonprofiteering and what we must achieve—and ways to get there—both now and in the future.

Most important, the book is a guide for the rocky path ahead. We're entering one of the most critical junctures in our sector and our nation's history. In the last quarter of the last century, we witnessed the Pyrrhic victories of trillion-dollar social programs, the demise of communism, the rise of global capitalism, and the failure of so many social and governmental experiments to create equality and wealth. We suffered the tragedy of 9/11 and along with it experienced the increasing anxiety over corporate globalization and domestic threats. We've been forced to question our trust in once hallowed organizations like the Red Cross and United Way, and, more profoundly, in our institutions of faith and our presidency. On top of all of this, we're also on the cusp of the largest generational shift in the country's history, with 74 million boomers approaching retirement and a startling lack of infrastructure or resource in areas of health care, food support, and financial security to accommodate this major tectonic shift.

So where do we begin?

We begin with the right attitude. We need to "grab the future by the face," as Joe Strummer of the Clash sang. We have to question why we keep doing the things we do even when they don't work. We have to see whether it's possible to do things better, smarter, faster, and cheaper. We have to begin not just looking for change, but demanding it. And we have to evaluate honestly and be prepared to let go of people, programs, and policies that no longer work, no matter how historic, politically correct, or politically connected they may be.

Someone once told me there are three types of nonprofit people: those who talk; those who do; and those who can talk about what they do. I fit into this third category, and this book is dedicated to my friends and fellow freedom fighters who can't sit back, shut up, or go with the flow. We want, expect, and demand more from inside the sector . . . and so should you.

Begging for Change is going to be a wild ride through a million different motivators. It's the story of giving and taking over the last 100 years, and the outlook for our next 100. It's about my city of Washington, D.C., your city, any city in the world.

It's about what we can do to make these cities better places for our future.

It's about you, me, us.

And it's about time we got started.

"Brother, Can You Spare a Dime?"

A Brief History of the Handout

They teach you to fix what needs to be broke.
—PAUL WESTERBERG

The men and women enrolled in the 12-week job training program at the D.C. Central Kitchen fight battles every day of their lives. They're fighting hunger in Washington, D.C. They're fighting a personal history of poor education and poor employment skills. They're fighting against low entry-level wages and tough commutes. They're fighting stereotypes of who they are and what they can achieve. And they're fighting against a society that wants to keep them right where they are, and a nonprofit sector that too often can't let go of them.

Not everyone makes it through our job-training program, but the ones who do learn about responsibility and hard work. They think independently and know how to work together as a team. Most important, they learn to be givers, not just takers. By the end of each training program, if the students come in on time every day, if they haven't failed one of the random drug tests, if they pass the final exam and walk down the aisle for graduation, they will have learned to wield the most powerful weapon in anybody's arsenal: the one between their ears.

Like the volunteers and employees at other innovative nonprofits around the country, the trainees at D.C. Central Kitchen represent a new breed of nonprofit fighter. Once the burden, they're now part of the solution. They're redefining the rules of engagement against social ills like homelessness and hunger, and winning battles against stereotypes and low expectations. They're taking the nonprofit sector to new levels of reward and success.

But in order to understand why these fighters are different from anyone before them, and how they're leading the nonprofit movement in a new direction, you have to better understand where we've been as a sector. As the saying goes, if you don't know your past, you're doomed to repeat it. And since the end of the 19th century, we've witnessed the same mistakes being repeated over and over again: lots of good intentions, but not a lot of real results.

Why has the practice of charity remained the same after all these years? How did the nonprofit movement get started? And how did "doing good" turn into a lucrative career path? Let's take a brief walk through the history of the nonprofit sector to see if we can answer these questions.

The Nonprofit Crusades

The modern nonprofit sector began in the late 19th century, when coal and steel magnate Andrew Carnegie and Standard Oil founder John D. Rockefeller wanted to use their business acumen and unparalleled wealth to address society's worst problems, such as hunger, poverty, poor education, and homelessness. At the time, the ideas of Social Gospel and social Darwinism were in vogue. So as titans of their industries and society, Rockefeller and Carnegie felt a moral, religious, and social duty to save the souls of the less fortunate. They were so convinced of this calling—and confident of the new tools of empirical science and American ingenuity—that they were willing to invest millions of dollars of their own money to finance this crusade. It was their version of noblesse oblige with teeth.

But these two men had little interest addressing the *symptoms* of social problems, as many charity groups and church-based programs had done for centuries. They wanted to eradicate the problems altogether. "Neither the individual nor the race is improved by almsgiving," Carnegie wrote in 1889. Rather than create more poor farms and poorhouses—by 1900, the Catholic Church was supporting more than 800 charitable organizations in the United States and teaching more than 1 million children in tuition-free parochial schools—Rockefeller and Carnegie wanted to get to the root of poverty. Rather than build new hospitals to treat the infirm, they wanted to fund researchers and institutions that would find cures for diseases.

Carnegie and Rockefeller wanted to shift the concept of "charity," a 4,000-year-old practice dating back to King Hammurabi of Babylonia, to a more modern Age of Enlightenment term known as "philanthropy," which sought to improve society as a whole rather than the individual. Their ideas seemed bold and fresh at the time, but they weren't exactly original. The general concept of philanthropy dates as far back as the "teach a man to fish" parable in the New Testament. Even in American history, two of our Founding Fathers, Benjamin Franklin and Dr. Benjamin Rush, had toyed with the concept of charity-cum-philanthropy 100 years earlier.

Franklin organized civic societies, work associations, and libraries that helped the hardworking citizens of Philadelphia get a hand up, not just a handout. Ever the inventive thinker, he explored uncommon ways for individuals to achieve self-empowerment and self-sufficiency in colonial Philadelphia, as he explains in this passage found in the essay, "Giving in America," by Robert Gross:

> If you teach a poor young man to shave himself, and keep his razor in order, you may contribute more to the happiness of his life than in giving him a thousand guineas. The money may be soon spent, the regret only remaining of having foolishly consumed it; but in the other case, he escapes the frequent vexation of waiting for barbers, and of their sometimes dirty fingers, offensive breaths, and dull razors; he shaves when most convenient to him, and enjoys daily the pleasure of its being done with a good instrument.

Dr. Benjamin Rush, a friend of Franklin's, embraced the same belief in individual self-improvement. A prominent doctor and one of the signers of the Declaration of Independence, Rush became the principal architect of prison reform in early America. Rush's guiding philosophy was not to punish the crime, but to cure the criminal. And by far his most famous achievement was Eastern State Penitentiary, an austere stone prison that symbolized Rush's thinking on the subject. Eastern State enforced a strict regimen of isolation and hard work (e.g., shoemaking or weaving). Prisoners were not allowed to interact with anyone else in the prison, not even guards, so that they would have the private time to reflect on their crimes and eventually seek penitence from God. For criminals who wanted to leave Eastern State, only the penitent man could pass.

Rush and Franklin enjoyed success carrying out their social experiments because they lived in much simpler times. In 1790, there were fewer than 4 million people in America. The City of Brotherly Love had only 22,000 residents. Life in a city was small and contained enough so that workers lived near their employers and often mingled with them after work. On any given street, you could turn to a neighbor or friend for a favor or a handout. Any failure to repay that debt would lead to ostracism from the small community. Thus, the face-to-face giving known as "charity" and the larger social agenda known as "philantrophy" could work together easily.

What made Carnegie and Rockefeller's vision so bold a century later was the size and scope of their endeavors. Rush and Franklin wanted to help Philadelphians. Rockefeller and Carnegie wanted to help the entire country, in some cases the entire world. By the turn of the 20th century, the U.S. population had grown 20-fold since Franklin's day: Philadelphia alone had a population of 1.2 million people. Wherever you found masses of people living together, you also could find disturbing cases of poverty and social disease. In northern industrial centers, blue-collar families lived in crowded, filthy shanty towns that lacked adequate water or sewage. Dead rats were often found floating in the water supply, and diseases were spread from shack to shack as quickly as a chilling wind. In more rural areas in the South, people survived on meager rations of corn meal and molasses.

Fortunately, with such great numbers came opportunity for great wealth. In the late 1870s there were only 100 millionaires in America, but by 1916 there were some 40,000 of them, many of whom felt the same religious and social conviction to give back some of their money to worthy causes. Like no other generation before them, Carnegie, Rockefeller, and other wealthy women and men such as Olivia Sage and Julius Rosenwald, one of the founders of Sears Roebuck, had the "Benjamins" to finance social reform on a grand scale.

Carnegie was so committed to the cause that he eventually sold his stake in Carnegie Steel in 1901 for $447 million in order to devote himself full-time to the business of philanthropy. He took delight in writing treaties and articles about the imperative of giving ("A man who dies rich dies thus disgraced," he once wrote), and personally oversaw the disbursement of thousands of grants, gifts, and endowments around the world. Over his lifetime, the Scottish-born former bobbin boy left an impressive legacy in his name: Carnegie Mellon University, the Carnegie Foundation for the Advancement of Teaching, Carnegie Hall, and the World Court Building in The

Hague. He helped establish public libraries in more than 2,800 communities (as a kid he had spent many hours reading in a public library), and even funded the purchase of more than 7,000 organs for churches around the country. Say what you want, the man had a vision. By the time of his death, Carnegie alone had distributed more than $300 million to philanthropic causes.

Rockefeller, meanwhile, never presumed to be an expert in giving, so he remained at the helm of Standard Oil and appointed a former Baptist minister named Frederick Gates to oversee all of his philanthropic operations. In doing so Rockefeller created the first foundation, and Gates became the country's first nonprofit director. Among his list of impressive accomplishments, Rockefeller converted a small Baptist school into the University of Chicago and established the highly respected Rockefeller Institute for Medical Research in New York. By the early 1900s, scientists at the Rockefeller Institute had found a cure for hookworm, developed a yellow fever vaccine, and lowered rates of infant typhus. Indeed, with such proud achievements, Rockefeller was pleased with the lasting results he was getting for his money.

As individuals stepped up their efforts to help the needy, so too did organizations. The turn of the 20th century marked the emergence of a new crop of public service groups around the country. Organizations such as the Salvation Army, Goodwill Industries, the YMCA and YWCA, and the American Red Cross were founded in the late 19th century; many were linked to ecumenical causes.

This rise in nonprofits also led to increased competition over local funding. To deal with this problem, national leaders in business and nonprofit decided that rather than have each nonprofit raise money in its respective community, there should be a "federated group" of fund-raising organizations that could raise money in a single campaign. This allowed each group to achieve economies of scale and divide its resources among many different agencies. Known as the Community Chest, this federation became the predecessor of what we know now as the United Way (and we *will* talk about that later). By 1929, there were 329 cities and towns with autonomous Community Chest chapters. All around the country, many nonprofit agencies were thriving.

The Great Depression, Soup Kitchens, and the Rise of the Nonprofit Bureaucrat

Under the guidance of wealthy philanthropists and religious-based charitable groups, the nonprofit sector basked in all the glories of its newfound success. People were fueled with the optimistic belief that social change could be engineered and attained. Even war, Carnegie believed, could be averted with enough research and study. In 1910 he established the Carnegie Endowment for International Peace. By the end of the 1920s, the endowment had commissioned hundreds of scholars to study the origins and preventable measures of World War I. As with so many of Carnegie's and Rockefeller's efforts, the endowment's 240 monographs were a testament to their belief in the science of philanthropy, believing as author Judith Sealander notes in the book *Charity, Philanthropy and Civility in*

American History, "If only enough facts were unearthed, if only root causes were explored, a solution to warfare could be found."

By the Roaring '20s, the first generation of philanthropists were aging out of the nonprofit sector. No longer able to handle the day-to-day demands of his philanthropic work, Carnegie joined Rockefeller in relinquishing his duties to foundation officers and grant officials. The transition from first-generation philanthropists to second-generation nonprofit managers marked a new era of growing bureaucracy and infrastructure in the sector.

But without doubt the most significant event of this period, an event that nearly caused the collapse of the nonprofit sector, was the Great Depression. We've come to associate this era with familiar images of hungry Okies, haggard-looking folks selling pencils on street corners, and of course the long lines of disheveled men waiting for a meal at a soup kitchen. During the depression, unemployment rates reached as high as 80 percent in some urban areas. Foundations and religious institutions were overwhelmed by the demand for their services and the scarcity of supplies and resources. Individual donations to churches and nonprofit agencies dropped to nearly nothing. Many local nonprofits were forced to shut down, and even the Salvation Army, perhaps the country's most established and stable nonprofit at the time, had difficulty paying its mortgages and employee salaries.

Before the depression, relief for the poor and unemployed had always been the responsibility of individual families, local governments, and private charities. Organizations like the Community Chest were opposed to the government's playing a role in serving local communities. But faced with impending collapse, these agencies welcomed Franklin D. Roosevelt's New Deal policies, which created temporary relief programs, established new governmental agencies, aided thousands of citizens, and employed thousands more.

In his first 100 days in office, Roosevelt enacted numerous changes intended to prop up the nation's sagging economy and buoy the public's sinking morale. He set up the Civil Works Administration, the Civilian Conservation Corps (to help employ people), the National Recovery Administration (to help with industrial production), the Federal Deposit Insurance Corporation, the Securities and Exchange Commission (to monitor financial institutions), the Agricultural Adjustment Administration (to help farmers), and the Tennessee Valley Authority (to provide public power and flood control). Near the end of his first term, he also established the National Labor Relations Board, the Works Progress Administration, and the Social Security Administration, which ensured an immediate flow of federal funds to the elderly and disabled.

FDR's administration was also responsible for creating new tax laws that gave businesses and private citizens incentives to donate more to nonprofits. Prior to the depression, few citizens or businesses paid income or personal property taxes. Most of the government's money came through trading tariffs. But the hard times of the depression led Congress to pass the Federal Tax Act of 1935, forcing companies to pay taxes on revenues. Business owners now had an incentive to find tax shelters and loopholes to avoid paying these fees. Some of them created tax-exempt incorporated foundations under the guise of "doing good." The Ford Foundation, for instance, was set up originally as a tax shelter and a way for Henry Ford to ensure the transfer of his publicly held company to his son, Edsel.

Then, at the start of World War II, Congress was forced to find additional funds to pay for the costs of war. Even though the Sixteenth Amendment, which gave the federal government the right to tax citizens, was ratified in 1913, elected officials were wary of abusing this power. Americans still paid nearly zero income taxes, and property taxes were minimal. But when Congress imposed universal tax rates on citizens, individuals, like businesses, had the incentive to contribute tax-deductible income to charities. Philanthropy as Social Gospel or noblesse oblige had shifted to philanthropy as a means to preserve wealth. Thus, FDR's administration had shifted the role of the federal government from a hands-off guardian of its people to active social agent. His administration's policies and tax laws also opened up new revenue streams for the nonprofit sector to grow. The era of "big government," as President Reagan would describe it years later, had begun.

Good Deeds as Big Business

By the 1950s there were 50,000 tax-exempt organizations in the country, so many that Congress decided to redraft the IRS law to classify nonprofit organizations into more than two dozen "501(c)" categories, including charities, clubs, cooperatives, labor unions, insurance companies, patriotic and veterans organizations, and political parties. Charitable, educational, and religious entities were eligible to receive 501(c)(3) status, which gave them complete exemption from corporate income taxes and allowed deductibility of all contributions. Other categories, such as lobbying groups and associations, were allowed tax-exempt status, but contributions were not tax-deductible.

During this time, nonprofit service agencies were still limited in the coverage and scope of their services, but they faced little competition for funding. Agencies that depended on the local Community Chest received 50 percent or more of their operating budget from this single group, while other organizations relied primarily on private donations or client fees. Even though the federal government had redefined its role as an active participant in society, few nonprofits received any federal funding at the time.

In the early '60s, President Kennedy asked Americans what they could do for their country by calling for them to "help our less fortunate citizens to help themselves." He wanted the government to play a more active part in trying to get individuals off the dole. "We must find ways of returning far more of our dependent people to independence," he told voters.

After Kennedy's assassination, Lyndon Johnson followed through with Kennedy's vision by declaring the War on Poverty. Believing the federal government could do for society what Carnegie and Rockefeller had tried to do with private philanthropy, the Johnson administration shaped federal economic policy and legislation that took advantage of the young boomer population, through such programs as the Job Corps, the Neighborhood Youth Program, and work-study programs for college students, while also thinking about the elderly and low-income citizens through such new creations as Medicare and Medicaid. Indeed, the initial antipoverty bill that Johnson signed in 1964 seemed to fit the ideas of empowerment and self-sufficiency. "The days of the dole are numbered," Johnson said.

LBJ used his political prowess to create his Great Society, which opened up new federal funds to a growing sector of social services. It also widened the nonprofit battleground by acknowledging an entirely new array of social issues. Before the '60s, most Americans had seldom thought of addressing problems such as senior care or rape crisis or domestic violence. Yet now thousands of liberal-minded, enterprising young people—inspired by Kennedy but mobilized by LBJ—were venturing into both new and familiar categories of social service.

By the mid-1970s, there were nearly 600,000 tax-exempt organizations in the country and more than 1.5 million people employed in social services in the U.S. The federal government had also become the largest single source of direct and indirect revenues for nonprofits. Even though the army of nonprofit soldiers had grown since the days of Carnegie and Rockefeller, so too had the face of the enemy. It had morphed into a million new forms, both visible and invisible, both understandable and totally unfathomable. Helping people was no longer as simple as the face-to-face act of giving a man a razor, as Ben Franklin had proposed long ago. Race-based policies and the politicization of even the most fundamental social issues such as housing and hunger contributed to more dialogue and less action. Every person had unique needs, and every agency served a unique set of constituents.

As the sector grew, the battle lines changed almost overnight. Organizations had to pick and choose not only whom to fight but whom to coordinate and partner with. But there were two big problems, ones that Johnson never imagined and nonprofits even to this day are struggling with:

1. There are no market forces or governing bodies to oversee, organize, and streamline the operations of nonprofits; and
2. *Everyone* wants to be a general.

Since the 1960s thousands of organizations in communities across the country have developed *their* strategies for winning *their* battles. Rather than working together to fight a common enemy, these fighting units have been scattered over the battlefield and tied up with their own skirmishes. Each agency began with enthusiasm, determination, and good intentions, but over time, many of them suffered from poor lines of communication and turf wars. They duplicated each other's services and fought one another for supplies and funding. Most important, for older organizations, bureaucracy had set in, and it had no intention of going away.

Back at the turn of the century, individuals like Carnegie single-handedly oversaw the performance and return on investments of hundreds of different philanthropic ventures. But today the modern field of charity and philanthropy is governed by hundreds of thousands of brains (and egos), many of them career do-gooders who've never run their own company or started their own successful agency. They include officers of billion-dollar foundations, local mom-and-pop foundations, department heads at local and federal government agencies, corporate philanthropists, university professors, and individual donors. With so many nonprofits fighting for limited control and resources, but at the same time accountable to a multitude of funders, what you have is a million field captains directing their own battles and taking orders from their commanders. And all the while they're jockeying other troops for a finite amount of ammo, soldiers, and silver stars.

The Propaganda War

Over time public confidence in the movement began to waver. LBJ's War on Poverty was not just failing to gain ground, it was *losing* ground. In 1968, roughly 13 percent of Americans were poor. By 1980 we were spending four times as much to eradicate poverty, but do you want to know the percentage of poor people? Still 13 percent.

During the '60s the White House conducted performance studies to determine the success rate of the Manpower Development and Training Act, a job-training program that was JFK's prized project. Studies showed that males who were in the program increased their earnings by only $150 to $500 in the year immediately following the training. And this amount actually decreased by up to 50 percent during the following five years. It was hardly the impact this multibillion-dollar program was expected to generate.

A more alarming study conducted by the Johnson White House in 1968 showed that only 50,000 of the 7.3 million people who were on welfare were capable of getting the training and skills to become completely self-sufficient. That meant less than 1 percent of those on the dole had the means actually to get off the dole.

In the last quarter of the 20th century, nonprofits began to use a language and display an attitude that almost excused their performance ("What do you expect, we're just nonprofits?"). Meanwhile, our fervor for social reform had become politicized, with organizations and interest groups blaming politicians or political parties for problems that all of us agreed had to be solved.

Rather than winning the War on Poverty, we focused on containing the enemy. Rather than looking for a solution, we found it easier to blame either a cause, a political party, or an economic system. As competition among nonprofits got ferocious, we tapped into advertising and public-service announcements to raise money. This quickly led to cause-based marketing and new partnerships. We teamed up with corporations whose only goal was to increase profits: "Buy this product and something 'good' will happen."

We regressed to a junior high locker-room mentality where size was the only measurement that mattered; we pointed to how many millions of dollars we could raise, how many people we sheltered, or how many meals we served, but avoided discussion of how this money was used, or how many people got out of the shelters or away from dependency on these meals.

We managed to convince our donors to focus on measurements like fund-raising efficiency (i.e., how much of a nonprofit's budget goes to fund-raising) and charitable commitment (i.e., how much money goes to the cause instead of overhead and management) because these were easy numbers to present. Yet we knew they didn't reflect the true impact, efficiency, or effectiveness of any nonprofit.

By the mid-1990s, we fed off the thriving economy and the seemingly endless supply of dot-com money. Businesses appeared infallible. The new mantra inside and outside the sector was that nonprofits should be run more like businesses. The captains of corporate America became the new high priests, and nonprofit executive directors took to using business buzzwords like "measurable outcomes," "donors as investors," and "creating capacity." As more people got rich, a new generation of nonprofit fighters transitioned from the corporate world to a nonprofit career that seemed to offer more meaning and purpose. Nonprofits began hiring these business veterans and paying them salaries commensurate with those in the private sector. A second mantra filled the air: You have to pay good salaries to get good people. Healthy six-figure salaries became the norm for nonprofits with mid- to large-sized budgets.

By the end of the '90s, the movement had grown again, totaling more than 1.5 million organizations. But more significantly, it marked the upgrade from the standard nonprofit bureaucrat to the *extremely well paid* nonprofit bureaucrat.

During this same period, we convinced thousands of young troops to postpone their corporate dreams for a tour of duty in the social service sector. We lured disaffected, but idealistic Generation Xers and Yers to join groups like AmeriCorps, Teach for America, or the Peace Corps. We established volunteer organizations to handle the millions of people who wanted to donate time and skills for a worthy cause.

Yet we were too busy and underfunded to give these

young men and women the proper training, mentoring, and support they needed to turn them into lifelong fighters. Who can blame them? We expected them to help us defeat an enemy we couldn't measure, spend investments that were hard to make honest returns on, and build to a capacity that seemed impossible to create. Even worse, their exposure to the bureaucracies of the sector left many too jaded to continue. Eventually, these young troops left the sector, either burned out or pissed off, while we scratched our heads, not understanding why.

It's been 115 years since Carnegie wrote his article "The Gospel of Wealth," 70 years since Roosevelt's New Deal, and 40 years since Johnson declared the War on Poverty. We've spent trillions of dollars in programs, expended millions of person-hours, and written thousands of pages of scholarship and research to figure out how to win this crusade against social disease and poverty.

What do we have to show for it?

Here in the District of Columbia, my beloved hometown and home to the world's most powerful policy makers, the cost of housing is too expensive for one out of four families. Four out of five high school students score more than 200 points below the national average on their SATs. One hundred thousand people live below the poverty line—a figure that is simply staggering when you consider that the District has only 580,000 residents.

I could pound on your head with more statistics, but what's the point? You're smart. You already know things could be better. And I certainly don't need to quote more numbers to make you see a light that's been glaring in our eyes for the past century. Wherever you live, you'll see the same patterns and the same social problems, problems of affordable housing, hunger, living wages, health care, and job training.

We don't need more numbers, studies, or statistics. We need a plan. We need to see things differently. We need less Cassandra and Pangloss and more Copernicus and Patton. We need to see as Archimedes did when he ran down the street naked shouting out, "Eureka!" We need independent-minded people who not only see a world through 21st-century shades, but know how to win on a 19th-century battlefield. We need people who can make the painfully truthful assessment that the greatest enemy in this crusade is ourselves—our outdated thinking and our outdated ways.

We have to think smarter, work harder, and never slow down. And we need to start by stopping first. We need to call a "national time-out" so that everyone around the country can ask themselves what the hell they've been doing and why. Only then can we begin again.

My Charity Crusade

As you'll read in the next chapter, I discovered soon after I started the D.C. Central Kitchen that winning my war—the war against hunger—wasn't just about feeding more people or building more-efficient kitchens. Even if I spent the rest of my life raising hundreds of millions of dollars for the "cause," I realized, all the money would never end hunger. Hunger is tied to other battles. It's about education, child care, job training,

AIDS work, drug counseling, affordable housing, and health care. It's about what products we buy, how we donate our money, and how we vote. It's about connecting with the people we're serving and partnering with others who share our vision. It's about creating a system of self-sufficiency for two things: the people we're assisting and the services we're providing. It's about building alliances with volunteers, donors, corporations, and other nonprofits that all share a unified vision of the future. It's about smashing stereotypes, fighting hypocrisy, and saying to everyone in your community, as Sly and the Family Stone said, "I want to take you higher."

You probably think these observations should be filed under D for "Duh," but you'd be surprised how difficult they are to implement in the nonprofit world. That's because over the past 50 years the structure of nonprofits has evolved for optimum survival, not optimum results. More and more agencies are fighting each other for a finite amount of public and private money and recognition, which means that most groups end up small, undercapitalized, and frustrated that they can't get ahead.

If you're only as strong as your weakest link, the nonprofit service sector today is for the most part a dangerously thin chain supported by a few enormous links. The largest nonprofit service organizations, such as the Salvation Army, America's Second Harvest, the United Way, and the American Red Cross, have revenues that run as high as several billion dollars a year, while foundations such as Ford, Bill and Melinda Gates, Kellogg, Carnegie, and Rockefeller have billion-dollar endowments that ensure their longevity regardless of how the economic wind blows. And yet more than 70 percent of the non-profits in this country have revenues under $500,000 a year.

At the other end of the spectrum, most local service agencies around the country face similar day-to-day battles involving budget, staff, and resources. They struggle to hire and train employees. They're stuck between paying high salaries to their upper-level managers and offering respectable wages and benefits for lower-level employees. Many don't have the financial security to plan long-term goals. Some have to cobble together dozens and in some cases hundreds of different grants and subsidies to run their organizations, all of which have strings attached that in some way compromise the mission. Every day they fight a battle of survival just to keep themselves running. So it's no wonder that people in the sector have such a hard time focusing long enough to think long term.

And yet the harsh reality is that some of these organizations shouldn't be running day to day. Many of them should go out of business, but because they're in what's called the "independent sector," neither the government nor Adam Smith's Invisible Hand has the power to make them go away. Whenever a nonprofit falls upon tough financial times or is accused of poor management or bad business decisions, it can and often does hide behind its charitable mission, as if doing good excuses it from being accountable and effective. If our sector were subject to the same forces as the for-profit sector, tens of thousands— maybe hundreds of thousands—of social service agencies would have merged, consolidated, or most likely gone out of business. Instead, they stay afloat because of lax IRS laws, an internal code of silence, and a public that hates to see an organization with a worthy cause go under, no matter how anemic it is.

And this is one of the biggest problems of the sector: We are perpetually helping perpetually failing nonprofits.

The nonprofit sector lacks what economists refer to as "creative destruction," the consolidation or destruction of the most ineffective and wasteful organizations. The only way to improve the nonprofit sector is for every constituency—the government, the private sector, the public, but most important, nonprofits themselves—to demand more and expect more from our nonprofits. We need to seek out and reward organizations that exemplify leadership, unity, responsibility, and accountability—and let go of those that can't or won't. We have to follow the leaders and organizations that have developed new ways to fight the war. We need to arm ourselves with what they're using.

We need their ideas.

Not just any ideas. Powerful ideas. Creative ideas. Ideas that inform, instruct, and inspire. Ideas that organize and mobilize. Ideas that smash stereotypes and empower individuals. Ideas you can take to work and use at home, in the classroom, in your place of worship, and in your relationships. Ideas that show you the connection between all of these things.

When we win the battle of ideas, the enemies that manifest themselves from bad ideas will disappear.

The rest of the book will focus on all the good and bad ideas I've come across in my lifetime. Chapter 1 will tell the story of how the Kitchen got started. The rest of the chapters will share some of the lessons learned about being in the nonprofit and nightclub businesses. Finally, the last section will provide a guide for evaluating and improving the field of giving. It may not contribute to a radical overhaul of the sector, but it will surely get the conversation going about where we need to go.

There have been a lot of books published on the topic of nonprofit management and reform. Too many in fact. The last thing I want to do is add yet another title to an already crowded category. But my approach and my point of view should offer a new angle on this subject. Trust me, *I'm not that smart.* (In fact, after the Kitchen was named one of President Bush's Thousand Points of Light, my wife, Claudia, liked to call me her "Dim Bulb No. 275.") But I'm sure as hell not dumb enough to repeat what we've been doing in the charity business for the past 115 years. None of us should. We've got too much to do and too many problems to solve. And besides, there's a generation behind us who'll be paying an enormous price if we don't start to get it right.

So let me begin by telling you about the city I'm trying to change and how I ended up here. People are always asking me how I got here. How did I go from running nightclubs to running a nonprofit? Did I have an epiphany that made me want to work with the hungry and homeless? Did I spend a dark night with my soul, or fall off a horse like Saint Paul?

No, I tell them, I got here on a truck.

CHAPTER 1

Soup Kitchen Confidential

Captain Renault: What in heaven's name brought you to Casablanca?
Rick: My health. I came to Casablanca for the waters.
Captain Renault: The waters? What waters? We're in the desert.
Rick: I was misinformed.
    —*Casablanca*, 1942

In my previous life, I'd been working in nightclubs. Ever since I saw *Casablanca* at the age of 12, opening the greatest nightclub was all I ever dreamed of doing. Rick's was the kind of place where you could fall in love, sing patriotic songs at the top of your lungs, or win your freedom at the roulette wheel. Risk and danger were as much a part of the menu as caviar and champagne cocktails. The owner never stuck his neck out for anyone—or at least he made it appear that way—but everyone stuck their necks out there. More than anything else, though, from the moment I saw *Casablanca*, I wanted to *be* Rick.

In the late '70s, while all my friends went off to college, I went to chase my dream. I landed my first gig at a cabaret and restaurant called the Fish Market in Old Town, Alexandria, Virginia, right on the Potomac. I spent my nights in the upstairs showroom—my first classroom, you could say. We had a one-eyed banjo player named Johnny Ford on the weekends, and a cross-dressing piano player who performed as "Herb" on Mondays and Wednesdays and as "Miss Vicky" on Tuesdays and Thursdays. And actually, except for the man-hands, Vicky wasn't, in the parlance of my father, a bad-looking broad.

At 21, I moved into D.C. and got a job at a popular club named the Childe Harold, right above Dupont Circle, where I became the bartender, manager, and eventually booker. The Childe Harold was one of those classic blues clubs of the '60s and '70s that was caught in the crossfire between the blues of old and the counterculture punk of new. It was the kind of venue where we booked Emmylou Harris one night, the Bad Brains the next. We had the Ramones for their very first gig in D.C. and blues guitarist Mike Oldfield for his very last (he overdosed a few days after the show).

Everything about the Childe embodied the holy trinity of the '70s club scene: sex, drugs, and rock and roll. I dove in with abandon and spent the next two years learning everything I could, which, as is often the case, is best summed up as "everything you shouldn't do" if you expect to stay in business, let alone stay alive.

In 1983, as punk morphed into new wave, and cocaine and AIDS hit us big-time, I had reached a point where I had to take my nightclub schooling uptown to learn the wants and needs of a richer clientele. I became the manager and maître d' of a jazz club named Charlie's, a swanky place named after the famous local jazz guitarist, Charlie Byrd, who had come back from Brazil in 1961 and, with Stan Getz, introduced the country to bossa nova.

Charlie's had everything going for it: a great location in posh Georgetown; a dark and modern, sort of deco, feel, with long, comfortable banquettes; a piano bar; a showroom in the back; and more than anything else, stellar entertainment. We had big name acts every week, with legends like Rosemary Clooney, Al Hirt, Mel Tormé, Sarah Vaughan, Billy Eckstine, Bobby Short, the Kingston Trio, and Astrud Gilberto, aka the Girl from Ipanema.

On Wednesdays through Sundays, I'd walk down to Charlie's in the late afternoon dressed in my own version of Rick's classic attire, a white dinner jacket and blue cowboy boots that my fiancée, Claudia, had bought for me in New Mexico. Four o'clock was My Hour, the hour before dusk. The French call it *l'heure bleu*. I was inside Charlie's, getting ready for whatever excitement or disasters were in store. The musicians and electricians would be setting up mics and instruments. The star of the evening would be dressed in casual street clothes to do a sound check.

At 7:00 p.m., it was "Showtime!" for the staff, and we were rolling. We pushed the standard supper-club high-ticket items—lobster, prime rib, surf and turf. The waiters pushed a lot of Dom and layered drinks on the customers to get the checks up.

Champagne out front, cocaine in the rest rooms, and everyone—men and women—smelling of Calvin Klein's Obsession. And lots of talk—Washington people tended to talk through the performers, even the top acts people paid a lot of money to see. After closing, Simon the Brazilian bartender and I would pour ourselves a little Rémy, count the receipts, and check the liquor stock. Then I'd cruise through the kitchen, watching as food servers tossed away unused fish, steak cuts, vegetables. Like other restaurants, we had little storage space. "Night, Amadou," I'd say to our towering North African chef. And then I sailed out the door and walked up the hill to my apartment.

So . . . about that truck that got me here. Well, when I trudged up Wisconsin Avenue from Charlie's, I'd always pass Grace Church, a 100-something-year-old stone chapel overlooking the Potomac River. Claudia and I wanted to get married, but we'd found most of the Georgetown churches fairly snooty except for Grace. The minister there was more than willing to marry us at an affordable price, so as a goodwill gesture, we started attending service as often as possible.

Grace was part of a volunteer effort called the Grate Patrol that, along with other churches in the neighborhood, took turns cooking food and serving it to the homeless at designated street corners. Being the new kids in the congregation, we were encouraged to volunteer for the Grate Patrol. But feeding the poor on a truck just wasn't my thing. Then one day we got cornered by an organizer and had run out of excuses.

On a gray, overcast Tuesday afternoon, I found myself in the teeny basement of Grace Church, helping other volunteers cook a mammoth pot of lentil soup. The goal was to feed 140 people in the District. We had white bread, the soft kind, cookies, oranges, and bananas. "No apples" we were told, since many of the "grate" people had bad teeth and couldn't chew. I'd never thought about that, but it made sense.

Around 6:30, as we sat out in front and watched the sun set over the Kennedy Center, a Salvation Army truck pulled up to the church. It was a renovated delivery truck with shelves and countertops spotted with coffee and food stains from the hundreds of runs it had made over the years. We filled 10-gallon Cambro containers (think really big thermoses) with soup and got inside, and the four of us—Claudia, me, and two veterans of the patrol—took off, riding standing up, bouncing over D.C.'s infamous potholes.

Frankly, I was nervous and a little bit scared, if not for me then for Claudia. She always wore large, dangling hoop earrings that I bought for her from the street vendors in D.C., and I warned her, "Baby, you should take off your earrings." I didn't explain why, but I thought to myself, What if some crazy homeless guy tries to grab them off you when you hand him his dinner? Claudia, who grew up in Albuquerque, New Mexico, and who could more than look after herself, rolled her eyes and politely suggested, in language I won't repeat, that I lighten up.

Our first stop was the corner of 21st and Virginia Avenue, right across from the State Department and near George Washington University. A light rain started to come down. As soon as we rounded the corner, I saw people had already formed a line. There were almost 40, mostly men, but a few women, and the way they gathered instinctively around the truck was almost Pavlovian. Some were lucid, some were babbling gibberish, some were scamming. "Hey, can I get some for my buddy?" Some flirted with Claudia.

Interestingly, we never left the truck. It was almost symbolic to me in a disquieting way, people reaching up to us, looking into our eyes, as we handed our gifts down. *God bless you, my child. Here's a bowl of lentil soup, now please step away from the truck.*

As we rode to the next stop, I asked the seasoned volunteers where the food came from. They told me that parishioners bought it at the Safeway in Georgetown and always prepared it in the basement kitchen. I thought about the incredible amount of food I'd seen thrown away in my career, but I was equally intrigued that the volunteers were shopping at the "Social Safeway" in Georgetown, probably one of the most expensive grocery stores on the planet.

At 17th and New York Avenue, across from the Corcoran School of Art and within eyeshot of the White House, an equally long line was already waiting. At the back was a guy in a suit with a briefcase. As he got closer to us, I saw that his outfit was frayed, and the briefcase was probably secondhand. Was this guy working, barely holding it together? Or was he a little "off," like the couple I'd see who pushed a doll in a baby carriage around the streets of D.C.?

The longer we stayed out there, the more questions I started asking myself. At every stop, the men and women threw their empties on the sidewalk and our driver would have to leave the truck to clean up after them. Many seemed to be down, but hardly out. Why weren't these people working?

Why, at least, couldn't they pick up after themselves? I whispered these questions to Claudia, but she said quietly in what now looks like a weirdly prophetic moment, "Robert, are you going to judge these people over a cup of soup? Besides, it's not our business."

But these questions were eating away at me. Was this all there was to it, handing out food? Where were the social workers, the homeless shelter partners, the drug counselors, the incentives to help these people get out of their situation, or at least out of the friggin' rain?

It certainly begged the most important question of the evening: Was the Grate Patrol part of a larger solution to end hunger in the District, or had it devolved into some kind of bizarre mutual dependency for the homeless and the volunteers? Who was getting more out of this exchange?

As we left our last stop in front of the World Bank and bounced down Pennsylvania Avenue back to Grace Church, Claudia noticed how quiet I'd become. I sat there amazed by the whole experience. I couldn't believe there were so many homeless people living in our downtown. Where had they come from and where did they go to at night? More important, why hadn't I seen any of them before? I'd grown up believing that anybody could pull himself up by the bootstraps, and I had heard the constant call from homeless advocates who protested to the Reagan administration that the homeless were just like you and me, but for the grace of God and our last paycheck.

But these folks who were being fed on the Grate Patrol *weren't like you or me.* Man, they were in *deep,* a whole hell of a lot deeper than a missed paycheck. They needed more than just a meal; they needed total life support. I couldn't help thinking that for all of its noble intentions, the system of feeding them every night was only helping them stay there.

The next afternoon, I was back at Charlie's, getting ready for another night at work, trying to focus on the business plan I'd been preparing for my own nightclub. And not just any place, but the world's greatest.

After nine years of managing clubs, I had decided it was time for me to turn my dream into a reality. My club would have a house orchestra and would put together original shows that would take advantage of the enormous talent pool in the area. I would combine original music, theater, art, and dance. The space would entertain locals, but also tap into the constant flow of tourists, diplomats, and lobbyists, spreading its name nationally and internationally by word of mouth and airwaves until, like Rick's, it was the only place to go in the nation's capital. Even the world.

And yet I couldn't take my mind off the truck I'd been on the night before. How could I just walk away from a hunger problem I knew I could help fix? Over the next couple of weeks, I talked with some colleagues in the food service—local chefs, restaurant managers, and friends who'd gone into catering—to see if they'd consider donating food to the cause. Each of them said that if someone could offset the liability issue so they wouldn't get sued for bad food, they'd be more than happy to donate their surplus. Hell, it would save them money if they could write off the deduction rather than throw the tons of food away.

Then I scheduled a meeting with the leaders of the Grate Patrol and a few local nonprofit execs, to talk about using the food more efficiently, and to test out an admittedly wild thought I'd had about the people I'd encountered that night.

The idea was simple: The nonprofits could take unused food that was thrown away by restaurants and caterers, but instead of dropping off this food at shelters, like a New York program I'd read about called City Harvest had begun doing around 1981, they could bring it back to a "central kitchen," where it could be chopped, combined, cooked, and then distributed. And instead of just cooking it, the nonprofits could teach the homeless people the basics of food service as part of a modest job-training program. To me, it was Food Service 101, a logic flow that seemed evident. *If you do this, this, and this, then you can do that, that, and that.*

"You can't take food from restaurants and feed people with it," one nonprofit director told me. "It violates D.C. health codes." I had similar responses from others I talked to. Some of them complimented me on an admirable idea, but seemed annoyed or amused by my naïveté. Even the parishioners connected to the Grate Patrol seemed ambivalent about the idea: "If we did as you suggested, we'd lose the fellowship of shopping and cooking together."

As annoying as these responses were, nothing cut me more than hearing the one concern that was repeated over and over again—a disbelief that homeless people were capable of anything more than just standing in line. "You want to train the homeless? Nobody will hire them." "Look, I know you mean well, but you're underestimating how hard it is for them to hold down a job."

This attitude put me over the edge. How could they stand by watching the recipients of the Grate Patrol take food day after day without any hope of getting out of that cycle? How could they not try to do more, or at least do it more effectively? I was stubborn—or stupid—enough to believe that I could prove them wrong.

So I put my nightclub dream on hold and decided to move forward with the kitchen. For the next several weeks, Claudia and I worked night after night drawing up a plan. I learned everything I could about nonprofits. I had a lawyer friend handle the legal work and create bylaws. I looked into the D.C. health code and saw there was no such law prohibiting the reuse of uncooked food. In fact, there were "Good Samaritan" laws in every state that protected people from liability if they wanted to give food to charity. The only thing I had to worry about was the time and temperature of unused food. Food couldn't sit out at room temperature for more than four hours, so I'd have to budget for a refrigerated truck.

I read all about foundations, corporate philanthropy, and other funding sources from books at the local library. I studied the application requirements and cyclical deadlines that passed throughout the year. Finally, after six months of research and hard work, Claudia and I sent out our first set of grant applications, along with a letter signed by 10 of my restaurant and catering friends pledging their support.

For the next several months, during the summer of 1988, I got rejection after rejection after rejection. Many were form letters; some were personalized with friendly well-wishes. I tried to keep my spirits up by telling myself that if a nightclub denizen and committed hedonist like myself could see the possibilities, and if my colleagues in the biz were as open to helping as they suggested, somebody in the nonprofit side of this coin *had* to be ready to buy in.

Then one day I received a letter from the Abel Foundation and saw, when I held it up to the light, the outline of what could only be a check inside. My heart raced. I was too nervous to look at the amount, so I tore open the envelope, tucked the check under my leg, and read the letter. "We have carefully reviewed your grant application and would like to inform you of good news . . . ," it began.

When I pulled the check out from under my leg, I saw the figure and nearly gasped: *$25,000!*

The next day I strutted into the bank, just like Steve Martin in *The Jerk.*

Twenty-five thousand dollars!

That's right, $25,000!

I'd made some dough in my day, but never all at once. To my young eyes, this was a fat check, and yet I knew it wasn't going to last me six months if I didn't spend it carefully. I also knew I wanted to avoid being dependent on what I was beginning to see as the whims and flavor-of-the-month funding policies of the foundation community. If I was going to leave my glorious nightclub vision, if even for a moment, I wanted to be damn sure I was not a slave of the system I had entered. I wanted to redefine, recharge, and rededicate the sector—not spend most of my hours drafting grant proposal after grant proposal just to keep the operation afloat for another six months.

To do that, I'd have to create some buzz around the venture. And I'd have to do it fast and cheap. That's where my nightclub experience began to kick in.

First I had to come up with a name for this thing. I'd toyed with a few ideas, but decided I didn't want to be too attached to a religious or political message. This wasn't a left-wing or right-wing thing. This wasn't a God thing. It was about feeding and empowering people. (Whenever people ask me if the Kitchen is a faith-based organization, I say, "Yes, we have faith in people.") The name had to be smart and accessible for everyone. That's when it dawned on me. If this was going to be a central kitchen, then so be it. We'll call it the D.C. Central Kitchen.

Once I had the name, I had to ask myself, How can I avoid the long march of selling this program over and over to funders and supporters in the community? I wanted the launch of D.C. Central Kitchen to have all the pomp and circumstance of opening night of a nightclub. Was there a way I could broadcast this message to the entire community all at once?

Then it hit me.

Vice President George Bush had just defeated Michael Dukakis in the presidential election, and being in D.C., I thought of a way to use this changing of the guard to my advantage. Reagan Republicans had taken a beating in the public eye for being perceived as rich, insensitive elitists. Knowing that Bush would want to counter that stereotype (his "Thousand Points of Light" speech suggested as much), I approached a friend who had been tapped to help the planning team for Bush's upcoming inaugural celebration.

"What if I came to every inaugural event with a refrigerated truck and took all your leftover food? I'll deliver it to local shelters and food programs, and you send out press releases. We all win." He loved the idea, and so did the rest of the inauguration staff.

On January 20, 1989, both the Kitchen and George Bush were inaugurated.

That night I drove all over the city, from reception to ball. I hauled steamship rounds of beef, trays of lamb, platters of shrimp cocktail, gallons of lobster bisque, and all kinds of desserts. I stayed out past 4:00 a.m. delivering the food from more than a dozen events.

The *Washington Post* ran an article about the D.C. Central Kitchen's grand opening, right below *Doonesbury*. Who could ask for better placement? Calls started coming in from journalists around the country wanting to cover the story for their publications.

Then I started getting unexpected calls. Instead of donors and volunteers who were dying to come help with our cause, I got calls from people who needed help.

"Hello . . . I saw that article and wanted to get some food for my family. Can you drop off a meal?"

"My mother is 85 and can't leave the house. Can you deliver her food?"

"My son's about to get out of prison. Is there a spot in your program when it opens?"

Calls like these forced me to rethink my view of hunger, which I now realize had been built from my stereotypes on the Grate Patrol. The face of hunger wasn't just those people who lined up every night for a cup of lentil soup. Hunger affected families. Generations. People with children, grandparents, working-class individuals, single mothers, prodigal children.

I also found a huge intellectual divide between the reality of the problem and the advocacy in the movement. Solving hunger wasn't about giving out a meal or spinning the issue to fit a conservative or liberal agenda. We could spend millions of dollars to expand meal services and advocate on behalf of the people we served, but we could never solve hunger unless we also found a way to help people help themselves. Food could never solve hunger, but it could be one hell of a tool.

As I started delivering food around the city, I began to recognize how nonprofits like after-school programs, homeless shelters, and senior centers have to deal with people every day, which means they have to deal with food issues every day. If the D.C. Central Kitchen provided these organizations with precooked, nutritious meals, these sister agencies would be able to keep more of their money, redirect their staff and resources, and ultimately stay more focused on fulfilling their missions. The same was true for individuals. Those single mothers or grandmothers who had to worry about feeding themselves could focus on their jobs or use the money saved to buy medication. The children who received an after-school meal wouldn't have to worry about the ache in their bellies and could concentrate on what their tutors were teaching them.

During the first year of the Kitchen, I forged relationships and alliances with restaurant and hotel managers, social service program directors, and homeless advocates. A $100,000 grant from UPS, given over three years, gave me the flexibility to hire another person and think of expanding services.

Since I hadn't found kitchen space, the majority of my time was devoted to picking up "rescued" food at 2:00 a.m. and then waking up a few hours later to deliver it to homeless shelters, churches, and community groups during the day. It was an exhausting schedule, like being on call every night, but luckily, the refrigerated truck had an external outlet that allowed me to pick up the food, park it behind my temporary office, and plug in the truck's refrigeration unit so the food could be left in the truck overnight. On some occasions, I'd return to find that a fuse in the truck had blown or a wire had shorted and the entire truck full of food would be spoiled. On one memorable evening, I pulled into my space at 4:00 a.m. after a late pickup and discovered the truck's extension cord that I'd snaked down from my office window had been redirected to an abandoned building next door. Inside the building were four homeless men, still up at this hour and using my juice to power up their appliances and radio. I cut a deal to give them some food in exchange for my extension cord. They agreed.

Then there was the night of a hundred pig eyes.

Pig eyes are tiny and intense, and one night I had 50 pairs of them staring at me from the back of a delivery van as I drove around Washington. They were attached to 50 suckling pigs that had been donated to my "soup kitchen" by the Smithsonian Institution after a poorly attended opening of an exhibit on the Caribbean. They sat in the back, lifeless but persistent, as I wondered how the hell I was going to convince our kitchen's chief chef, Abdul, a practicing Muslim, to cook them. That was one of the many late nights I asked myself what the hell I was doing, and why I wasn't running a warm, inviting nightclub where you didn't have to depend on the kindness of strangers. I wondered how my life in Casablanca had transformed to life in Bedford Falls.

Even to this day, whenever I get frustrated with the business of charity, I like to remind myself of "the night of a hundred pig eyes," and the willingness of people to bend barriers in order to help the hungry. Those suckling pigs were one of the best meals Abdul ever served, though he never tasted a drip.

By the time we celebrated our first anniversary I had secured a free home in an old kitchen at Fourth Street and Florida Avenue. It was underneath a community hall, and badly in need of renovation. For years it had served the black community of segregated Washington. By an odd twist of fate, my new office was where the bar used to be, and it was where musical riders of the "Chittlin' Circuit," who performed at the nearby Howard Theater, used to frequent between matinee shows. I was, it would seem, still in the biz, albeit tangentially.

One month later I hired a man who turned out to be my first and favorite intellectual partner in crime. Chapman Todd had been working at another "soup kitchen" for about six months, and like me he'd grown weary of seeing the same homeless guys coming in for a meal day after day, without any hope of ever getting out of their cycle of dependency. Over the next eight years, Chapman and I worked with other great colleagues to create something that no one had ever seen before. We went from two guys driving around D.C. in a truck to a team of people tackling one of the biggest social issues in our city.

As the program grew, every bump along the way taught us how to improve the ride for future trainees and employers. We developed a decent reputation in the city and attracted a surprising number of visitors who wanted to learn about our efforts to train the "unemployable." In order help other job-training programs in other kitchens around the country, we knew we had to develop a standard curriculum. So in 1991, we collaborated with students from the Cornell School of Hotel Administration to come up with a standard 12-week food-preparation and culinary program.

Why 12 weeks? We wanted a program that was more demanding and more instructive than a seminar, but not as rigorous as a cooking school. We also knew that many of the trainees had flunked out of school or at the very least had trouble following a textbook. Rather than create a book-based classroom that would set up many of the candidates for failure, we created a more hands-on learning environment. We invited local chefs like Roberto Donna, Jean-Louis Palladin, Nora Poullion, and Jose Ramon to come into the kitchen to demonstrate cooking and cutting techniques. We also took the trainees on field trips to local kitchens, like the one at Georgetown University, to see large-scale food service in operation. At the end of the 12 weeks, each graduating student earned a D.C. Central Kitchen diploma.

Early on in our adventures we discovered that our certification alone wasn't enough to certify our graduates as qualified workers. So we began to ask the trainees to take a District of Columbia certified food handler test, a $40 exam that allows each graduate to walk into any restaurant in the country with a piece of paper proving he or she has kitchen skills. During each training program, we hammer the rules of food safety and food prep to ensure that everyone passes.

"What's the safe temperature of pork?" one of the instructors shouts out to the class.

"One sixty-five!"

"What's the danger zone?"

"Forty to 140!"

I was shocked with the first class, when a few of the trainees passed the Kitchen's clinical tests, but failed the D.C. certified test. Turns out they were illiterate and couldn't read the written exam. All of a sudden, we realized we had more than just kitchen skills to test. We had to incorporate a reading quiz at the beginning of each training program to ensure that every student had basic literacy skills.

There were other major obstacles we had to jump over. But without a doubt the biggest one to hit us was the introduction of crack to D.C. With drugs like heroin, PCP, and alcohol, you could detect a person's path of self-destruction and try to cut it off before it got the best of the user. But crack was something else, the "devil's candy," as one of the trainees called it. It could ruin people's lives overnight. During the first year crack hit the streets of D.C., we noticed many of our supplies at the Kitchen were disappearing. Then one of our delivery vans was stolen, right around the same time one of our trainees disappeared from class. Police called us days later, having found the van in a strip mall parking lot . . . in Florida.

We also noticed that not as many trainees were graduating, and not as many graduates were holding on to their jobs. In response, we decided to expand our training program to do much more than just teach kitchen skills. We had to start teaching life skills, too. We hired a full-time counselor and job coach, and devoted two classes a week to job retention and held Alcoholics Anonymous and Narcotics Anonymous group sessions. We also implemented random drug tests. Anyone who failed a test had to leave the training class, no exceptions, but he'd at least be referred to another social program in D.C.

Every problem I could have imagined about working with

the homeless came true, though not always with the expected outcomes. I'd get calls in the middle of the night from trainees in a moment of crisis, needing a ride to a detox center to clean up. I'd come in to work on a Monday morning to find out that one of the trainees or a friend we'd met in one of the sister programs had been stabbed to death or had fallen from a building or walked in front of the bus after getting liquored up. One graduate was strangled to death, her killer never found.

Yet for every tragic story there were many more uplifting ones. Trainees who'd been kicked out of the program after failing a drug test would appear again months later clean and ready to reenter the program and graduate. Graduates who disappeared from their restaurant jobs (what we called "the second-paycheck syndrome") would show up at my door nine months later after having found a job on their own. Then there were individual stories I'll never forget, like Karen, a graduate of the Kitchen who asked me to officiate at her wedding with her fiancé, who like her had been living on the street just years before (my powers vested in me by the Universal Life Church through the World Wide Web). The wedding was held in the backyard of their home in suburban Maryland.

At every turn we bobbed, weaved, took some hits, but we always came back for more. In 1992, we moved into the larger kitchen in the basement of the Federal City Shelter, which housed an incredible 1,500 temporary residents. Located just two blocks from the Capitol, it had the right space and equipment for us to pick up momentum as an organization. It was cold and cramped in the winter and hot and cramped in the summer, but I loved it because, like the first kitchen, we got the space for free, utilities included, in exchange for food, training, and public services to the community. We added two freezers and four walk-in storage spaces.

We helped found Foodchain, a new national association of similar food recovery programs, which eventually merged with America's Second Harvest. We founded Kitchens, INC (Kitchens in National Cooperation), a Web-based association that allowed us to bypass the bureaucracy and costs related to building a national association. Kitchens, INC gave participating community kitchens around the country a free way to share ideas and opinions over the Internet. They'd ask questions like "How are you dealing with crack?" "How are you using food efficiently?" "Where are you getting free equipment?"

At every step, we shared ideas, helped each other build capacity, and fought the images that so pervaded the debate about social problems in America. But our attempts to create unity weren't enough to offset the larger battles in the sector. Sometimes, more often than we should, we fought each other and fellow players. We began to elbow each other over resources. Some began to cut corners in an effort to keep their machines alive.

As I traveled around from city to city helping open new kitchens that used D.C. Central as a model, I witnessed the rise of the nonprofit clone wars, where multiple programs were springing up, each fighting the same fight, but inevitably competing with one another over turf, funds, and public and government favors. Everywhere I went, the patterns were the same. In New York, there were 35 food pantries and kitchens in 1983; in 2003 there were 967. In D.C., there are approximately 25,000 nonprofits, and every year they have to raise more than $1.5 billion *just to pay the salaries of their CEOs and executive directors.*

Another disturbing trend I witnessed across the country was the "field of dreams" attitude about scale and size. People in the sector—and particularly the funders from the foundation and corporate community—believed that "if you build it, they will come." That is, if you create more agencies, more shelters, more kitchens, more food pantries, you can serve more people, and more is better. But the logic works for only half of the equation. The bigger-is-better mind-set brings in more clientele, but it does nothing about getting them *out of the system*. Where's the mechanism that enables people to free themselves of their cycle of need and dependency? Where's the strategy for building an exit that's as big as the entrance?

My partner Chapman asked these same questions when he worked at a street-feeding program in D.C. "See you tomorrow," Chapman would say to the "regulars"—the homeless people who would show up every day for their free meal. Why had it become routine to see the same homeless people stuck in the system with little hope of getting out? Whose field of dreams did these programs serve?

Leaders and researchers in the nonprofit sector want the public to believe that our lack of progress in the sector is caused by insufficient money and resources, and that we could do more if we could build bigger entities and more nonprofits. They're totally wrong. We don't have a shortage of funding or volunteerism. We're the most generous and caring people in the world. Nearly 90 percent of the population donates to charity, on average about $1,600 per household every year. And every year Americans donate around 15.5 billion hours of volunteer time, worth an estimated $239 billion in services.

In the D.C. area alone in 2000, individuals gave $5.4 billion to charities, and grant makers and corporations handed out another $1 billion. It's not that we have to say yes more often, or reach deeper into our pockets. We have to do the opposite. We have to learn to say no. We have to ask tough questions of organizations who are asking for a grant or a contribution. It's no longer about dollars raised, or percentages of money that go to the cause. It's about effectiveness and results . . . but it's also about fewer programs getting more of the money.

As I became more aware that the battle to end hunger—frankly, the battle to end any social injustice—called for change from the inside out, I also realized that there were too many people on the inside who didn't want change. Without an invisible hand or free-market system that could demand improvement and efficiencies in the sector, nonprofits were willfully, blissfully ignorant of the ineffectiveness of their efforts. No one wanted to question the organizations. No one was forced to look for a better way. In a manner that resembled medieval feudalism, nonprofits remained content with the status quo, focused less on winning the war and more on preserving people, money, and power.

Once, when we visited a community in the Midwest to help open a new community kitchen, a person from the local hunger movement told us, in a defensive tone, "We don't want you stealing our hungry people."

I found that the only way to combat the entrenched attitudes in the sector was to challenge them directly, even if doing so alienated me from colleagues or entire organizations. I wasn't in this business to be loved. I was in it to change things.

So rather than try to shape myself into the mold of a nonprofit executive, I borrowed from my nightclub experience to throw a little sizzle into my work. I questioned, poked, probed, and talked a lot more than people were accustomed to. I learned that much of what was being written about by academics and nonprofit "experts" had limited practical value and that the best models of advocacy and nonprofit management were the ones being practiced, not talked about. I learned about replication—creating a model that could be used in other communities—and the superiority of acting and doing to thinking and telling. Talk is cheap. Those who can do, should.

Over the years, I developed a good understanding of what works and what doesn't in the sector. The fundamentals of nonprofiteering aren't based on surveys or studies. They're not part of any academic or government trend. Rather, they're based on hands-on experiences in the trenches, seeing things work beautifully or blow up in our faces, and never being discouraged enough to give up. They're based on an entrepreneurial spirit to try anything, anywhere, without reservation, with the goal of achieving independence in every sense of the word— for the nonprofit, for the clients and community we're serving, and in our attitudes about all of the above.

The following chapters will tell you more about what worked and what didn't in my experiences at the Kitchen. I'll also draw from a few lessons I learned running nightclubs. It'll be a candid look at the good, the bad, and the stupid in the nonprofit sector—the things that have never changed and the things that have to change.

I didn't have to go far to find my first example.

CHAPTER 2

Doing Good Versus Doing Right

Anything not worth doing well is not worth doing.
—WARREN BUFFETT

There's a program in D.C., a revered nonprofit, that's been raising funds to open its second "permanent home" in less than six years. During the last capital campaign, this group raised more than $5 million to build a modern center to serve its constituents. But rather than buy the building, the group signed a lease and pumped $5 million into the facility. Most donors gave generously because they assumed they were contributing to a long-term home for the cause. And it is a good cause. I gave money to the campaign.

But wouldn't you know it? The building's property owners opted to cash out at the peak of D.C.'s real estate boom. The organization was forced to raise additional funds, $7 million this time, to buy land and build a new state-of-the-art center. The math is simple: When completed, the cost of finding "new" homes for this organization will have taken over $12 million out of our community.

The program serves a worthy cause. Its daily roster of 1,100 constituents is at the top of everyone's list of people who merit community services. But is the space for any local service agency worth $12 million?

How many other programs didn't get funded or struggled because of these capital campaigns? How many great ideas had to be put aside or abandoned because of this organization's lack of foresight and the community's unwillingness to ask questions or better yet to confront such poor planning? Did the organization really need to build a brand-new space, particularly when the economy is stretched so thin that many other deserving nonprofits are at risk of losing their own leases or falling behind in renovations that will keep them in operation?

Unfortunately, we'll never know the answers. The leaders of the organization were shielded from criticism because, like other nonprofit organizations, they could hide behind a noble mission. It's as if questioning the soundness of their planning is, in effect, questioning their integrity, their purpose, and the need of their constituents.

I'm not implying that the board of directors or the management didn't try to correct the situation in the best interests of everyone involved. And I'm certainly not suggesting that donors would have redirected the same amount of money to other causes in our area. What I am saying, however, is something basic: You can't get something for nothing.

If you tap into a donor pool that's also feeding thousands of other organizations, your consumption will affect the well-being of everyone else. Nonprofits committed to a common cause have to recognize the interdependent nature of their relationship with other nonprofits and the sector at large. We can't survive with an "every man for himself" attitude. In the nonprofit sector, we should take only what we absolutely need and demand that others act the same.

I'm faced with a similar dilemma at the Kitchen. We've been in the same basement space for nearly 13 years, using equipment that should have been replaced years ago. Building experts say we're going to need to pump in about $4 million to keep the space functional for another 10 years. Or we could run a capital campaign for more money to find or build a new space.

Let's say we decide to launch a $4 million to $5 million capital campaign for a new location. What would be the cumulative impact?

On the positive side, we'd have the money to get really smart and buy a flash freezer to keep food from going bad. There's never a shortage of fresh produce, but a flash freezer would help prevent spoilage. Additional funding would also allow us to expand the kitchen space and buy new equipment, which would allow us to make more meals every day and expand our reach to partner agencies around the D.C. metropolitan area. We could open a credit union and grow our for-profit catering unit, Fresh Start. We'd also want to build our job-training program to bring in more students, and we'd have to accommodate this expansion by buying one or two new delivery trucks and hiring a few more staff members.

Sounds great, doesn't it?

Now let's look at the flip side. The most obvious result is that we'd be taking money indirectly out of the nonprofit community. Organizations would have to scramble that much harder to find money in an environment that's already intensely competitive. And no matter how good they are at raising money, these nonprofits would probably have to make some compromises with their missions in order to survive.

Even if only 25 percent of our capital campaign ended up in the hands of other service organizations instead of funding a new building for us, that amounts to $100,000 grants to 10 separate nonprofit agencies—enough to keep a small program running securely for more than a year. Or it would mean two $500,000 grants that would allow two larger organizations to have financial security for several years—which would allow them to plan and strategize more effectively, which would in turn allow them to carry out their mission more successfully. Is a new state-of-the-art D.C. Central Kitchen worth more than the survivability of 10 worthy agencies? Can we do without a new kitchen for one more year? Or, as Spock asked Kirk, don't the needs of the many outweigh the needs of the few?

Now let's think about the worst-case scenario. By initiating a capital campaign and taking money from the donor pool, we might directly contribute to the downsizing or shutting down of sister agencies whose missions are integrally linked to the cause of fighting hunger. This could mean anything from layoffs at a drug treatment center that refers recovering addicts to our training program, to reduced hours of service at a community center or an after-school program that helps the very people we're trying to feed. So while we might go into the capital campaign thinking we're expanding the Kitchen as a better service to the community, our actions would have the exact opposite effect. We'd end up reducing our effectiveness by the very act of trying to improve it.

Experts in social policy call this the "law of unintended consequences." I call it "good intentions gone bad." Just because you're doing "good" doesn't excuse you from doing things smart, or doing it right.

When I took on the interim directorship at the United Way in D.C. in 2002, the chapter was mired in controversy. The previous CEO had committed a cardinal sin for a nonprofit by losing the trust of his donors. Under his direction, the organization had held on to donated money that should have been distributed to D.C.-area agencies. He had also hired nearly 40 new employees at a time when the payroll should have been tightened, approved a lucrative monthly consulting contract for his predecessor, and spent tens of thousands of dollars renovating his office. National newspapers created a public feeding frenzy by running articles exposing these ethically questionable practices. The public was outraged. Corporate partners like Lockhead Martin, Marriott, and even the Washington Redskins were backing out of their long-standing relationships with the United Way. And the worst aspect of this controversy was that local agencies in the D.C. community who relied on United Way funding were going to get screwed because of the actions of this one executive and the board of directors.

While colleagues, for-profit titans, and a few fellow nonprofit executives sat by watching the United Way of D.C. go down in a ball of flames, I decided to take the helm because I knew how important it was for the community. The United Way of the National Capital Area channeled donor money to hundreds of organizations, including the Kitchen. Without its support, we never would have been able to expand the D.C. Central Kitchen's services to include a job-training program or our for-profit catering division. And yet there were foundations in the D.C. area who actually had the temerity to exploit the demise of their local United Way in their annual fund-raising campaigns (e.g., "We're not like the United Way"). Like an old man who feeds the birds in the park, the United Way might have gotten a little shortsighted and fat around the middle, but that was no reason to kick it while it was down. If this organization went under, so too would many of the organizations who relied on its monthly checks.

The first thing I did upon arriving at the UW was set my salary at $85,000 a year. It was a huge pay increase for me because I'd been making $55,000 a year at the Kitchen, but a lot of people were surprised, given the fact that the average annual salary for the head of a UW chapter is more than $200,000. "Take at least $150,000," I was told discreetly by some UW insiders and even a few D.C.-based nonprofit directors. Then I heard there was grumbling at other UW chapters. If I took $85,000 at the second largest United Way chapter in the nation, how did that make *them* look?

But think about it. Here I was entering a United Way chapter that was suffering a serious image crisis. The United Way of D.C. had broken the most sacred covenant of any nonprofit: the trust of its donors. Like so many nonprofits, the

United Way exists solely on the goodwill and hard-earned dollars of the public, and yet it had practically flouted people's expectations for accountability and ethical responsibility. It's as if years of being stewards of the public's money and being in the business of doing "good" had made it unimpeachable. It's an attitude that, unfortunately, many of the older charitable institutions in this country have taken on over the years.

Why was I stubborn about this lower salary? I knew as soon as I filled my position at the United Way that I'd have to release more than 30 employees from the bloated payroll. Agreeing to a salary of $85,000 rather than $150,000 or $220,000 would be the difference between keeping a couple of midlevel or frontline employees rather than firing them. Sure, I could have gotten a higher salary, but would that have been the right thing to do?

This is all about setting an example for your employees, your donors, and especially your colleagues in the sector. The organization was suffering from a leadership vacuum, and leadership has to come from the top down. What you do as an executive director, whether through your own actions or your organization's, reflects on the entire pool of individuals and agencies who are fighting alongside you. Your behavior has an impact on all of these constituencies. It can be a shining example, or an embarrassment for your entire sector.

Case in point: In 2002, the *Washington Post* ran an article detailing a crisis in the growing number of hungry children in D.C. A well-known local philanthropist read the article and wanted to do something about this problem. He contacted a local hunger organization and told them he wanted to help raise a million dollars to help feed hungry kids. But like many big-time donors, he wanted impact with this money, so he and this organization came up with an overly ambitious summer program that gave a meal to any child who was enrolled in a D.C. government-sponsored summer program. Nearly *20,000* kids would receive one meal a day during the week and then a bag of groceries to take home every Friday afternoon.

The plan was built on good intentions, but one glaringly wrong assumption: The cost to implement this type of blanket policy would be incredibly high. The program sounded good, looked good, and felt good, but was it smart and practical? Could some of the resources have been used to help other programs or feed other areas of the population?

Few people would have known about this program except that eight months after it ended, the philanthropist came up short on his financial pledge, forcing the District of Columbia government to make an emergency grant to pay the remainder of the bill. In the tightest fiscal year of the past decade, the D.C. government had to allocate more than a half million dollars to clean up someone else's mess. The *Washington Post* ran an article detailing the mix-up, making the endeavor appear as yet another amateurish and inept attempt by the nonprofit service sector to "do good."

Is it any wonder that people think nonprofits should be run more like businesses? Will the public be as willing to contribute its time and money to the hunger movement? We'll never be able to measure the total damage or unintended consequences of this project. But what we know for sure is that it could have been managed better. And in the end, no one looked good.

Don't get me wrong. I don't want you to think that all

nonprofits are poorly managed or are always at fault. The demands of donors often put nonprofits in a compromised position. Understandably, nonprofits are skittish about confronting donor demands, even when they're presented with the most unrealistic or self-centered agendas.

Service nonprofits, as a whole, are up against innumerable obstacles that make it a challenge to get the proper funding, leadership, and personnel. And it doesn't help that foundations and local and federal governments have created a system of funding that creates havoc for all of us in the nonprofit sector. We experienced this firsthand at the Kitchen about 10 years ago.

During the mid-1990s, we were in discussions with the Department of Labor and the Department of Housing and Urban Development (HUD) about funding the Kitchen's job-training program, which prior to this point had been privately funded. We were eager to expand the program and were attracted to the notion of steady income via government grants. But HUD had tied its funding to a system that reimbursed programs based on the number of men and women who enrolled in a program, and the number who subsequently graduated and got jobs. The parameters sounded good in theory, but in practice our partner agencies—the drug treatment centers and homeless shelters that depended in large part on these types of federal grants—had more of an incentive to refer as many people as possible rather than enforcing strict guidelines on who was physically and mentally ready for the Kitchen.

We'd spent the first few years at the Kitchen coming to understand this delicate process of taking someone off the streets and eventually training that person to find and keep a full-time job. It involved many steps, like rungs of a ladder. First you had to get a person off the streets, then into a drug treatment center and a group house or supportive housing, then into a training program like the one at the Kitchen, and finally into a full-time job. These steps had to be taken slowly, one at a time. If we took someone at the ground level, who hadn't made it successfully up the first few rungs of the ladder, who didn't have the "clean time" or the life skills to get through the job-training program at the Kitchen, we'd just be setting him and ourselves up for failure.

Yet because of the HUD regulations, the sister agencies we worked with had every reason to play the numbers game and refer as many people as possible. The more people they referred, the more money they'd receive from HUD. But we knew it was a lose-lose proposition.

Then we talked to officials at the Department of Labor, who insisted that all men and women who benefited from Labor funding receive no less than minimum wage for their work (a policy that allowed the government to count these people as part of America's growing labor force). But we couldn't disagree more with this policy. The Kitchen already paid its trainees a $50 a week stipend, enough to ensure they could get back and forth to work and buy incidentals if necessary. But for many of the people we were dealing with, people transitioning from welfare to work, it would be too much too soon to start handing them $200 to $300 checks every week. Many of them were still in shelters or had just graduated from a 30-day drug treatment program. The Kitchen program had to be about learning real skills, not a check, and learning how to handle the responsibilities of handling cash without being sucked back onto the streets. We knew from experience that "too much too soon" was a formula for failure. Graduates of the Kitchen sometimes disappeared from full-time jobs after the first few paychecks. They'd end up back on the streets, having fallen off the ladder. And the only place for them to start over again was that first rung.

We weren't pleased with the HUD or Labor regulations, but if we walked away from these government grants, we'd have to turn to the foundation community. It was a pick-your-poison dilemma. By the mid-1990s D.C., like every city, was being over-run by new nonprofits. The foundation community seemed to be almost intoxicated by the concept of helping new nonprofits. But there were a few catches. Many of the 50,000 foundations in America wanted nonprofits to become independent of their grant-making cycles within a short time span of a few years; not a lot of these foundations offered grants of much more than $25,000 a year; and many of these funds came with strings at-tached that hindered an organization's operational abilities.

As a result, nonprofits have to cobble together dozens if not hundreds of grant proposals and donations to pay for even their most basic operations. One nonprofit, for example, gets its $20 million annual budget from 161 separate sources. Think about the infrastructure and staff required to generate and maintain that kind of funding network. It's not surprising that many nonprofits can't build toward capacity or achieve scales of efficiency, since they're too busy writing new grant proposals, updating quarterly performance reports, and finess-ing the relationships with officials from these foundations and corporate partners.

Recognizing these potential pitfalls, we saw a Faustian bargain in front of us. We could sign a deal with the feds to adopt a formula that encouraged overcapacity and mediocrity, or work like a dog for small foundation grants that would never allow you to reach capacity. What we faced was the crux of the funding dilemma that so many nonprofits have to deal with.

So what did we do? We had to find the middle path. Or as Johnny Cash said, "We walked the line." Recognizing the dangers of spreading ourselves too thin across too many donors or depending too heavily on one source, we wanted to keep our funding similar to an investment portfolio or a mutual fund, with a manageable group of diverse funds.

It took a lot of back-and-forth, but we negotiated with the feds to create exceptions to their guidelines. We also secured just enough foundation money to tweak our program and experiment with new intake and job-retention strategies. To this day that's how these programs are funded. We still maintain a diversified portfolio of funders so that we don't have to cater entirely to any one group. If any one of our funding sources drops out or loses its budget, we won't be forced to fold. Also, we began a revenue-generating catering business to help offset some of the expenses of running the Kitchen.

By spreading out our funders and "walking the line" with each of their demands, we've been able to ensure that our rung of the social ladder remains stable and secure. We're only one part of the equation in solving problems of poverty, hunger, and homelessness. The day we begin to think of ourselves as more vital than other agencies on the rungs above and below us is the day we fail ourselves, our clients, and our fellow nonprofits. We're all in this together, as parts of a larger ecosystem of giving and serving. We need to start thinking and acting together if we are to have any hope of making our efforts work.

CHAPTER 3

Feeding the Tapirs

The next time you want to blame someone, walk a mile in their shoes. That way you'll be a mile away, and you'll have their shoes.

—ANONYMOUS

Every morning on my way to the D.C. Central Kitchen, I'd walk down the hill from our home in Mt. Pleasant, through beautiful Rock Creek Park, and up another steep hill toward Connecticut Avenue. I'd take this route unless it was too hot in the humid summer months or too freezing in the dead of winter. Out the door by 6:45, on the Woodley Park Metro train by 7:15, and through the back entrance of the Kitchen by 7:45.

I loved my morning commute because it gave me a chance to cut through the National Zoo. At that hour, the animals are just beginning to stir, turning a quiet park into a cacophony of strange, wild sounds. The wolves are howling, the singing dogs of New Guinea are singing, the seals are barking, the gibbons are shrieking. Every morning I'd take pure delight in being able to experience a natural wake-up call. I'd think, How many other people in the world have a chance to hear these noises on their way to work?

As I'd climb up the hill toward Connecticut Avenue, I'd stop to say a quick hello to the most unusual animals in the park, the tapirs.

Tapirs have the snout of an anteater, the body of a large pig, and black and white stripes that zigzag at crazy right angles across their bodies. I'll never forget the first time I heard their shrill cry. "What makes *that* sound?" I asked myself. I followed the noise to the tapir pen.

It was love at first sight.

The tapirs were so odd looking, yet so mellow and well-mannered, that I easily took to them. I often stood by the fence marveling at how creatures this strange and this docile could have survived the demands of evolution. It wasn't long before I became a regular visitor to their pen.

I amused my friends by swearing that the tapirs would spot me coming from a distance and cry out to me with their nasally calls. I'd attempt to mimic their whistle, too, or if nobody was around, press my face against the fence and talk to them.

"How are you lovely ladies doing this morning? Sleep well?"

Then one day a friend of mine called up with some disturbing news. A zookeeper in Oklahoma was badly hurt while trying to feed a tapir. It dragged her into its cage, tore off her arm, punctured her lung, and scarred her face.

This was seriously shocking information. I felt like a parent who's just learned the class bunny killed a kid. How could a tapir do such a thing? It was the pencil-necked nerd of the animal kingdom. I grabbed the copy of the morning paper and confirmed the news.

Wow, I thought. Just when you think you know someone . . .

Lesson learned. I'd made assumptions about the tapirs based on what I had wanted to see in them: friendly, tame, and good-natured. Luckily, I never had to pay the same price as the poor zookeeper in Oklahoma. But the lesson was unforgettable nevertheless, and the story of the tapir has stuck with me during my excursions through the nonprofit sector.

The lesson? Don't feed the tapir.

The tapir is my number one enemy in the fight against hunger. Ask anyone else at a nonprofit and he'll agree. The biggest problem in the sector isn't a lack of funding or resources or volunteers, it's wrong impressions and stereotypes. Plain and simple. It's the attitude people have about who's hungry and homeless and "needy" in America.

Survey your friends, your relatives, your co-workers. Ask them who's hungry in this country, why they're hungry, what nonprofits are doing about the problem, and what we need to do to end hunger once and for all. I guarantee you'll start to see a destructive pattern of stereotypes dominating the dialogue.

At the Kitchen, we have to fight false impressions every

day, starting first with the volunteers. All volunteers start with at least one or two misconceptions about what they're getting into. They might be nervous because they've been told that they are going to be working in the basement of the country's largest homeless shelter or that they're using donated food. Right off the bat, we know they might be thinking one or all of the following: It's going to be dark and dirty; there will be big pots of stew or gruel simmering on dirty stoves; it'll be disorganized and crazy; and for heaven's sakes, there will be homeless people running around . . . with knives!

It's our job at the Kitchen to dispel these stereotypes as quickly as possible. You can't begin cooking without a clean surface, and you can't begin to implement change in the sector until you can clear the mind of stereotypes. Our job is to check everyone's mental bags at the door. Start with a clean slate.

Over the years I've seen the ways in which stereotypes play out across the entire nonprofit sector. The most recent example happened to me when I was interviewing for the interim directorship at the United Way. The board members I met with asked the kind of questions you would expect from a review panel. I demonstrated my understanding of the issues, my passion for the organization, and my willingness to jump into the fire they had inadvertently stoked.

But as we ended the interview, I was told by one of the interviewers that I was a great candidate, but not exactly a "CEO type."

I was floored. Here I was running a $5 million operation at the Kitchen. I had been making a payroll for 14 years. There were close to 60 cities running programs based on our model, and they didn't see me as a CEO? "What does a CEO type look like?" I wanted to ask.

Now, as you know, I got the job, but I was told that my days of blue boots and blue jeans were over, and that I should go out and buy a few suits. What does a suit have to do with leadership, ability, purpose, resolve, and stamina? Absolutely nothing. It just reminds us that we need less fashion and more passion. We're all about the Salvation Army, not Salvation Armani.

"Sure thing," I told them, and thought to myself, While I'm out I'll buy a few ties, since ties can be used as either a tourniquet or a noose, and by the end of my term at the United Way, I'd need one of them or both!

Once you start to stereotype, you spend more time assessing blame than solving problems. Everyone is guilty of this: Nonprofits use stereotypes to raise money or fight policy. Politicians use stereotypes to cut back on government spending. The public uses stereotypes to decide whom to support. No matter how you slice it, stereotyping has a way of hurting everyone and helping no one.

Let's spend a moment to talk about the issue of jobs and fair wages because it happens to be one of the hot-button subjects of stereotypes. People should understand: There is NO such thing as a *bad job*. There are lots of bad-*paying* jobs, and we can talk about that all day long. But I've heard countless nonprofit, foundation, and liberal colleagues wax on and on, and demean entry-level jobs as dead-end, burger-flipping drudgery. They blame greedy corporations and create an atmosphere where entry level isn't good enough for people.

Now, I won't argue with the fact that corporations are greedy and industries do have a way to go when it comes to wages. In fact, I'll be the first one to criticize companies and institutions that have poor employment policies. Harvard University, the most respected learning institution in the world, is one of them. They teach our best and brightest, the future leaders of our country. But what we don't know is what they teach outside the classroom, a valuable life lesson called How to Screw Your Employees 101. In 2001 Harvard found itself in a public controversy when administrators couldn't find the money to pay its janitors a $10.25 hourly wage that was comparable to the city of Cambridge, Massachusetts. As we'll discuss later, wages do matter, especially for an institution that is sitting on top of a $19 billion endowment.

But this argument is different from saying these janitorial positions are dead-end jobs. Think about what happens when you pay someone who's come out of a program like the D.C. Central Kitchen. When you have a person who has never worked before, who has limited education and often a history of substance abuse or incarceration, that person's first job should be celebrated. It's like the first 30 days of sobriety. There's a long, long road ahead, but you have to celebrate the early steps to create stamina and belief in the future.

Many of our grads *want* that first job at the local fast-food joint, even when we could have placed them in a different place. They have pride in the uniform. They want the scheduling opportunities. And where does that nonprofit leader come from trying to talk down to them about the work they have to do to put food on the table? Again, all jobs have worth, all jobs are important, all jobs have value.

When it comes to battling issues at the Kitchen, this discussion falls into one of the two most consistent forms of stereotyping that I've found both inside and outside the sector. These stereotypes are Blame the Victim and Blame Society:

1. Blame the Victim. This ideology plays into the subtle prejudice most of us have, but won't deal with when it comes to people in need. We use terms like "these" or "those" people, as in "All these people need is a hand up." It sounds honest and pious, but it implies that "they" are inherently weaker than we are, and if we just offer some help—as in a good kick in the ass or tough love—they just might be able to make it. This approach plays to those who feel or think or believe that in America, if you can't make it, you're lazy, shiftless, worthless, or a bum.

People who think these thoughts aren't bad people. Quite the opposite. They have been raised by families or in cultures that can't understand the idea of not working, not earning, or not participating. They distrust anything that suggests this isn't the way to live, and it's easier to think the person on the receiving end is simply malcontent. Why else would he or she choose to stay homeless, get pregnant, or smoke crack?

2. Blame Society. This ideology openly suggests that the cards are so stacked that it's impossible for people at the bottom to get on top. It implies that the entire system is flawed or corrupted, and that the Man will always hold down those who are less fortunate. It also suggests that donors and volunteers who subscribe to this view are somehow smarter, somehow more tuned in to the plight of, or more at one with, the victims. They

are able to comprehend deep thoughts. They *get it,* while the ones who don't are insensitive and cruel louts.

This attitude of superiority or enlightenment is packaged as caring. Volunteers are made to feel guilty that through their very existence they're keeping a person or a family or a race of people down. They stage "urban plunges" to see what it's like to be homeless for a few days or hours. They protest against faceless corporations and declare evil anyone or any company that doesn't openly demonstrate compassion.

Like the Blame the Victim camp, there's a shred of truth to the ideas of the Blame Society group. There's enough legitimacy in their beliefs to corrupt their thoughts. And it's that very righteousness that comes from a sense of legitimacy that makes the group dangerous.

Effective nonprofit leaders look for the right compromise between these two forms of stereotypes. They look for truths that lie on either side, but never stray far from the middle path in between. They know that while there's plenty of blame to be passed all around, there's also too much work to sit around blaming other people.

Let's stop pointing fingers and start using our hands to shake things up. Let's stop building larger pens for our ideas, and stop feeding the tapirs.

CHAPTER 4

Starfish and Random Acts

I'm a very good man, I'm just a very bad wizard.
—THE WIZARD, *The Wizard of Oz*

I n order to get beyond "doing good," you have to be organized and determined. But the most consistent message I've heard in my area of the nonprofit sector is the opposite. And it comes to us in a story about starfish.

You might have heard the story of a wise man strolling on the beach one morning. He sees thousands of starfish, swept in with the tide and stranded on the sand. Farther down the beach he sees a young man tossing them back into the sea. The old man approaches, and asks, "What are you doing?"

"The sun is up and the tide is going out. If I don't throw them in, they'll die."

"But son, there are miles and miles of beach and thousands of these starfish. You can't possibly make a difference."

The man throws another starfish into the water and shouts, "It made a difference to that one!"

I've heard this story a hundred times at fund-raisers or charity events. And I can't tell you how much I dislike it and how dangerous it is to the future of the nonprofit sector.

The starfish story promotes a certain type of giving, the random act of kindness. There's nothing really wrong with random acts. You should try to perform them every day of your life. Hold a door open for a stranger. Let someone pull in front of you during rush-hour traffic. Smile at the next person you meet.

But we run into serious problems when people start to confuse random acts of kindness with a social strategy. Simply put, our neighborhoods, our communities, even our nonprofit infrastructures, have grown too complex to rely on starfish throwers. What you end up with is too much or not enough.

Nothing illustrates this point better than disaster relief. In 2000, I was asked to fly out to New Mexico to help with the food assistance for a wildfire in Bandelier National Park, near Los Alamos. The fire had been raging dangerously close to residential neighborhoods, and as a result the national news had been covering the event, which created a lot of public attention. The day after a thirsty firefighter happened to mention the need for water on TV, a truck arrived filled with bottles of water from the good people of Reno, or Wichita, or El Paso. Another day one of the firefighters mentioned that a good number of animals had been captured and placed in local animal shelters.

Wouldn't you know it? Trucks pulled up filled with pet food and pet products—more than anyone could handle or store. We joked with the firefighters that one of them should appear on TV asking for meatball subs.

The point, as I've said before, is that we're incredibly generous as a society. We give more than we should when there's a natural disaster or a tragedy like 9/11. But this generosity comes at a price. Before the fire in New Mexico was even contained, we ended up having to give away or throw away a lot of perfectly good donated supplies for lack of storage or need. We give too much randomly and not enough strategically.

When it comes to the day-to-day work that nonprofits perform, if we are to have any hope of creating lasting change in our society—the change that Rockefeller and Carnegie wanted—we have to turn to organization and strategy, not random kindness.

More specifically, we need to look to exceptional nonprofits who know how to motivate, inspire, and guide these starfish throwers and turn them into organized agents of change.

The March of Dimes is one these exceptional organizations. It is one of the first nonprofits to successfully organize a nationwide, mass-appeal fund-raising campaign. Founded by President Franklin Roosevelt with the goal of assisting victims of polio and funding researchers to find a cure, the March of Dime's annual fund-raiser was a nationwide dance held on FDR's birthday. With the slogan "Dance so that others may walk," these dances were successful enough to raise $1.6 million in small donations in 1938–39.

Then in 1950, the March of Dimes launched its Mother's March Campaign, which enlisted female volunteers to go door-to-door in every major city in the country. In 1954, their efforts paid off. Jonas Salk, whose research was funded in part by the March of Dimes, discovered a cure for polio. The March of Dimes not only converted starfish throwers into organized fund-raisers and donors but also used these resources to fulfill its mission of eradicating polio.

A more recent example of lasting impact involves a group that's trying to solve a problem that plagues every community: foster care. Every year, 20,000 of the nearly 600,000 foster children around the country are forced to leave the security of foster care. Studies have shown that one out of four of these kids experiences homelessness, fewer than half of them find and keep jobs, and 60 percent of the young women get pregnant. Many of them suffer from poor education and life skills. One foster kid, for instance, had lived in a group house all his life. By the time he was 18, he didn't even know how to operate a phone, since all of his outgoing calls were dialed for him at the front desk.

Business and religious leaders in Orange County, California, were concerned about the lack of a safety net for the foster children who were aging out of, or "emancipating" from, their local system. These leaders asked a simple question: How do you go from helping an individual foster child—a single starfish—to creating a system that helps many of the 250 to 300 youths who emancipate every year in Orange County?

To find the answer, members of the Mariners' Church in Irvine partnered with the Orangewood Children's Foundation to create a nonprofit called Rising Tide. The members of Rising Tide decided that the only way to get foster kids on the right track was to make sure these youth had an intermediary step between foster care and independent living.

"We recognized that the first problem you have when the kids emancipate is that they have no place to live," says Dick Gochnauer, one of Rising Tide's founders. "And because they have no place to live, you lose track of them. And once you lose track of them you can't help them anymore. If we could solve the housing problem right off the bat, then we could serve the community, and help the kids become fully functioning members of society."

Gochnauer and his colleagues had to find a reliable source of housing for these kids, one that would help them learn the skills to survive in the real world. Rather than strike a deal with a shelter or an affordable housing project, their ambitions ran deeper. They bought their own 80-unit apartment building and set aside 10 of these units to house up to 18 former foster kids. They also hired a full-time residential counselor to live at the complex and help advise and mentor these young residents.

Using the real estate and financial expertise of its volunteers, Rising Tide was able to finance the purchase with low-interest bonds, foundation grants, and bank loans. By renting the remaining units to low- and middle-income residents, the members were able to create a business model that brings in enough revenue to maintain the property, pay the counselor's salary, and subsidize the costs of Rising Tide residents. New Rising Tide members get their first month's rent free, pay $100 for the second month, and then gradually increase their payments until they are paying near market value at the end of 18 months. Along the way, the mentors and counselors at Rising Tide help the youths find jobs, learn day-to-day responsibilities and social interaction skills, and even set up a dollar-for-dollar matching savings program up to $50 a month. Rising Tide has purchased a second apartment community and plans to continue looking for more housing locations once they work out the kinks in their system.

None of this would have been possible without the organization and teamwork of Rising Tide's church members and civic leaders. Rather than saving a single foster kid—or starfish—Rising Tide has organized its efforts to try to serve nearly half of all foster kids in Orange County. That's making a real difference in their community.

The March of Dimes and more recently Rising Tide are examples of organizations that have demonstrated an ability to organize individual goodwill and acts of kindness into real change in their communities. Every once in a while throughout history, however, we come across individuals exceptional enough to create this sort of impact on their own. The Reverend Martin Luther King Jr. and Mahatma Gandhi rank up there in this category.

We all know the story of how a 42-year-old seamstress named Rosa Parks was arrested for refusing to sit in the back of a segregated bus in Alabama in 1955. But did you know how the black community responded? Through organization . . . and a lot of dimes.

During the two days after Parks's arrest, members of the Montgomery black community, led by a local pastor named Martin Luther King Jr., met to discuss a plan of action. They decided to rally the black community of Montgomery to boycott public transit. Even though the fares were only a dime, the leaders knew that if enough of the 17,500 black commuters who took the bus twice a day boycotted the system, the dimes would add up. Over the next few days more than 40,000 leaflets were printed and distributed around the black community calling for a boycott. Black ministers urged their congregations to stop taking public transit. It is estimated that 90 percent of the black community participated in the boycott. They took "black only" cabs, arranged car pools, and walked. Some even rode on mules to get to work.

Think about it. The entire power structure of the city of Montgomery was aligned against them. The press, the police, city hall, the courts—all were bent on thwarting the boycott. Hell, if you get down to it, the entire state of Alabama and the southern infrastructure were against them. The black leaders of Montgomery faced harassment, false arrests, and terrorist bombings, but they persevered. A year later, with the boycott still going strong, the U.S. Supreme Court declared Alabama's segregation on buses illegal.

Martin Luther King Jr. and the March of Dimes proved that even with something as small as a dime, you can create a profound impact helping others. It's not how much you have, it's how you use it. Mahatma Gandhi, another one of my heroes, also proved this maxim in his protest of British occupation of India, only in his case he used something as common as salt.

In the early 1900s the British government controlled a monopoly on the sale and distribution of all salt in the Commonwealth of India. Even though table salt was readily available in India—and vital for one's health in such a hot climate—the British banned the production and use of any salt not sold by the government. In 1930, Gandhi decided to lead a 200-mile march across India to protest the Salt Act and British occupation. His plan was to walk to the coastal village of Dandi and take salt from the waters of the Bay of Bengal in a symbolic act of defiance. He said to a friend before departing, "Supposing 10 men in each of the 700,000 villages in India come forward to manufacture salt and to disobey the Salt Act, what do you think the British can do?"

Gandhi began his march with 78 fellow protestors. Along the way countrymen and -women joined his protest. By the time he reached the village of Dandi to scoop a symbolic handful of mud and salt from the sea, his fellow protestors stretched behind him for nearly two miles.

Gandhi has been referred to as the father of India's independence. Indeed, his actions, like King's during the Civil Rights movement, were instrumental in bringing about the emancipation of an entire people. And these seismic changes started with something as simple as salt or dimes, combined with leadership and organization.

Groups like Rising Tide remind us that impact runs at all levels, whether it's a community organization trying to put an end to a serious social problem or a national organization in pursuit of finding a cure for a disease. Impact even applies to a single family donating to a local agency. It's a matter of doing the most that you're capable of doing, as we are reminded in the parable of the widow's mite in Luke 21:1–4:

And he looked up, and saw the rich men casting their gifts into the treasury.

And he saw also a certain poor widow casting in thither two mites.

And he said, Of a truth I say unto you, that this poor widow hath cast in more than they all: for all these have of their abundance cast in unto the offerings of God: but she of her penury hath cast in all the living that she had.

At the Kitchen we put it another way. We say, "It ain't what you got, it's what you do with what you got."

A few years ago, I was speaking at a fund-raising event in D.C. One of the photographers shooting the event approached me afterward and told me that he and his wife and 9-year-old daughter make 50 sandwiches a week for the Kitchen and bring them in every Sunday. Chris was downright humble about his efforts. "I hear they go to an after-school program, but I don't know if it makes a difference," he said.

"Are you kidding me?" I answered. "*Of course* it makes a difference." He and his family were supporting many amazing things. First, they were making 50 meals a week that we at the Kitchen knew we were going to get and could plan ahead for. That helped us divert our resources to other needs. Second, the meals were for an after-school program that allowed kids to recharge physically before their tutors arrived. Third, the kids' parents, many of whom had just left welfare for their first jobs, could focus on their work, knowing their kids were safe and fed after school; and with that focus came the skills they needed to earn a raise, which would translate into more independence from social programs.

We could go on here, but there's the most important point of all. I love the fact that he and his wife were getting their daughter involved in public service at such an early age. He and his wife were teaching their daughter about the difference between charity and responsibility. Studies have shown that adults are twice as likely to volunteer for a charity and are more generous givers if they volunteered as youths. That's impact.

I thanked Chris and told him how much we appreciated his efforts, knowing that he was going to go home feeling energized about his efforts and that he'd spread this energy and goodwill to his wife and daughter.

It reminds me of when my term began at the United Way, and I drove around the area as often as three or four times a day talking to disgruntled donors. Keep in mind, the typical United Way donors are the heart of middle America. They're making maybe $35,000 to $50,000 a year (average household income in this country is slightly higher than $50,000) at businesses that have supported the United Way for decades. A lot of these people came up to me saying, "I've given generously to the United Way, but now I'm not going to give you another cent!" I couldn't blame them for feeling this way.

Why give to the United Way instead of giving directly to the charity? For that matter, why give to any federated organization? Why not make sure your dollars go straight to the cause by donating directly to an individual charity?

Why? Because giving directly to charities is akin to saving starfish. Think about it. There are more than 1.5 million nonprofit organizations out there. We can't all survive if we have to depend on starfish throwers. I told thousands of disgruntled donors a personal story from the Kitchen. I said that if I had to wait at my mailbox every day for random donations, I'd either be out of business in my first year or still handing out cups of soup in front of the World Bank.

Thanks to the steady checks from the United Way, however, we not only stayed in business, we could plan ahead to find ways to serve our clients better in the future. The reliability of these United Way checks arriving on the 15th of every month made all the difference for a young organization like the Kitchen.

Another problem with giving directly to an organization is that these types of designated donations usually come with strings attached. Individual donors would rather see their money go straight to the cause, not to expenses like administrative overhead. Yet it's the administration that allows an organization to be more effective and efficient in carrying out its cause. The American Red Cross, for example, outraged donors when it wanted to use some of its billion-dollar 9/11 Liberty Fund to create an emergency cash reserve and to build infrastructure for its blood network. Why hadn't the Red Cross already established this kind of system? people asked. Because so many of its donations come restricted, which makes it hard to pay for the infrastructure necessary to create an efficient blood network. If we nonprofits are supposed to act like businesses, we have to be funded like businesses. That means having the freedom to do what we have to do with the money—with few strings attached.

If you're going to give time or money to charity, try to have an impact with what you do. Rather than spreading your checks and your volunteer hours thinly around, try sending all of your money or devoting all of your time to a single organization or cause. Believe me, it'll make a difference for the recipient. If the government and foundations did this, rather than dispersing their grants in thousands of directions, we might be able to gain some ground in this war. The same strategy applies to you.

Sure, the United Way and the Red Cross aren't perfect. Sure, there's a lot of waste and overspending at these institutions. But we can't abandon these institutions in favor of anarchy. As Churchill said of democracy, it stinks, it's a failure, but compared to the alternatives . . . Or as my great-grandfather, who was the mayor of Louisville, Kentucky, liked to say, "You don't shoot the horse just 'cause it's thrown a shoe." Even though we all had problems with the way the Red Cross handled the public's money after 9/11, we still had a duty to keep donating blood—and I can proudly say I am a 12-gallon donor.

No matter what role you play in the sector, whether you're a donor, a volunteer, an executive director, or a fundraiser, you can't contribute to any real impact in helping others with random acts. Be a starfish thrower in your spare time, but don't turn your nonprofit or business into one. You have to be smart and organized to win this war. You have to have long-term planning, long-term action, and the ability to mobilize the idea of starfish throwers into machines of social change.

Just ask Chris's daughter. She'll back me up.

CHAPTER 5

Whom Are You Serving?

If you have come to help me, you are wasting your time. But if you have come because your liberation is bound up with mine, then let us work together.

—LILA WATSON, Australian Aborigine, in response to mission workers

When the antihunger business really got rolling in the 1970s, the primary method used to distribute food was the food pantry, where staff or volunteers handed out bags to men and women who were on welfare and, for the most part, unemployed. They had all the time in the world to come to the pantry, wait in line, and carry home what was given to them.

The face of hunger has changed considerably since then. In fact, national groups like America's Second Harvest (A2H), the U.S. Department of Agriculture (USDA), the Food Research and Action Center (FRAC), and Bread for the World cite recent statistics indicating that the typical hunger profile is a working woman with two kids (nearly two-thirds of adult emergency food recipients are women). She has always worked, or has recently left welfare and is trying to make do on her own. This woman gets up in the morning and gets the kids out of bed, dressed, and off to school or to the sitter. She's running to catch a bus or driving through traffic to get to work on time. It's probably her first job and she's trying to get by on $7 to $10 an hour. By the end of the day, she's hustling again to pick up those kids.

Now, we know that on $10 an hour, which is as good as she might make in many job markets around the country, she's *never* going to get to the end of the month without help—especially when you consider that the living wage in a city like Washington, D.C., is over $16 an hour.

Not only do we know this woman's going to need help, but when we're out raising money, we tell everyone who will listen about how hard it is for this woman, and how she shouldn't have to choose between food and rent, heat, or medicine. Yet we still rely on pantries to meet her need: pantries that usually open a few days a week between the hours of 9:00 a.m. and 2:00 p.m.

Think about it. Here's a woman who has to bend over backward to make ends meet, who's doing her best to fight a system that's stacked against her. But the pantry she wants to turn to doesn't even open before she has to be at work, and then closes before she gets home. The very program that was designed to help has become a barrier. Not only have we in the hunger movement failed to meet our client's needs, we've officially become part of the problem.

The situation brings us back to the question I had asked my first night with the Grate Patrol. Were we really out there to help the homeless, or were we fulfilling our own personal needs?

Whom were we really helping?

My friend Bryan Eagle asked the same question in 1998 when he created a nonprofit business incubator for his town of Memphis, Tennessee. An MBA with a prior career in the telecom sector, Bryan had been following the huge success of dot-com incubators, but wondered why "empowerment zone" incubators in economically underdeveloped neighborhoods were struggling. These empowerment programs, many of them federally funded, were designed to give residents in low-income areas a chance to become small-business owners in their own neighborhoods. As Bryan found out, many of these programs set themselves up for failure by easing the restrictions and guidelines on who was eligible for a loan. Rather than setting up a mentoring or apprenticeship system to guide new business owners toward economic prosperity, these programs focused on handing out money and getting out of the way. But unfortunately, the skills needed to cut hair or mow lawns aren't the same skills needed to run your own barbershop or a lawn care business. Many of these neighborhood businesses shut down within the first year of operation. In most communities, the incubators or empowerment programs also disappeared.

Bryan wanted to avoid falling into the same trap with his

incubator. So with $4 million raised from the local community of Memphis, he set up Emerge Memphis with a thorough screening process for new applicants and a comprehensive follow-through plan for each fledgling company. And he had to be tough by rejecting a lot of applications that didn't have strong enough management teams. Bryan recognized that even though his nonprofit incubator would create new social services and jobs in the Memphis community, he couldn't lose sight of the business side of the venture. It served no one's interest to accept companies that were destined for failure.

Under his program guidelines, each new company receives anywhere from $50,000 to $100,000 of startup funding, free office space, and clerical support. Most important, each company gets "adopted" by a board member who has the business experience to mentor it through its first few years.

Today Emerge Memphis has 21 businesses in incubation, one-third of which are nonprofits focused on the economic development of certain sectors of the city. One company that "graduated" a few years ago from the incubator has $10 million in sales revenue. Bryan would love to bring more new companies into the incubator, but he knows that what's important is not how many businesses get created but how well they do in the long run.

Whether you're starting a business incubator like Bryan, working for a nonprofit, or just volunteering your time, you should constantly ask yourself whom you're serving. Where are your priorities? With your clients? Your donors? Your employees and volunteers? Yourself even? Who matters most?

The most effective nonprofits find the connection between purpose and effort by identifying the priorities of those they're serving. Unfortunately, in some cases, workers, volunteers, and donors don't always see things the same way. They can get caught up in their own personal beliefs and needs, as I'll illustrate with a few stories from the Kitchen.

Over the years the Kitchen has had to deal with an entire contingent of volunteers and hunger advocates whose primary goal is to change the eating habits of the poor and hungry by serving them healthy, nutritional meals. We even have a name for them: nutritional imperialists.

Now, I'm all about feeding people healthy food. Without a doubt obesity and its related health risks pose one of the greatest problems of the future for this country—hell, for the entire world. We need to use less Sara Lee and more cerebellum or we're going to be overwhelmed with a health crisis that will spread across entire generations of global citizens.

But that doesn't mean we should try to turn everyone into vegans overnight.

The truth is, most of our clients aren't crazy about nutritional food, especially vegetarian meals. The people we serve are Americans, and, I'm sorry to say, Americans love their meat and starches. Take a look at the kids we serve. The Kitchen makes meals for dozens of after-school and weekend youth programs. We learned that if you give the kids a meal of healthy food—e.g., eggplant lasagna, salad, and an apple—they won't eat a thing. Kids will be kids. They'll take one look at the plate, pinch their noses in exaggerated disgust, and walk away hungry.

But if you give them a slice of pizza—which we always have thanks to donations from local pizza chains—and you put the pizza next to a healthy salad, and a good piece of fruit and a cookie, they'll practically lick their plates clean. Once they see the pizza and cookie, they suddenly see everything else on the plate as edible.

Nutritional imperialists will come into the Kitchen with thoughtfully prepared meals that might include hummus, carrot sticks, and peanut butter—foods I personally enjoy. As much as I appreciate their efforts (unless they're pushy about it), I have to ask them a simple rhetorical question: Which is better? Giving kids a full healthy meal they won't touch, or a decent and respectably healthy meal that they'll eat and come back for? It brings up the question of whom you're serving. If you can't answer that question without qualifying your answer, you need to reevaluate whatever you're doing.

The same goes for volunteers. One time at the Kitchen a woman I'll call Lisa called our volunteer coordinator, Ed, and told him she was coming down to the Kitchen to help out. She never asked if the day and time she had planned was okay with him. She just assumed he was desperate for help and would take whatever he could get. She also said she had some computer skills and was willing to help out in this area. This woman was in her late 30s, a corporate type who worked in the technology sector in D.C. But when she came down to the Kitchen, she never tried to find Ed or get an orientation. She just started working in the kitchen. Ed finally noticed her working and also saw that she wasn't getting along with the trainee she had paired up with. He was trying to show her the proper way to pick apart a turkey, but she had the attitude of "I'm doing this how I want to do it and I'm not going to listen to what you have to say." She was becoming visibly angry, so Ed moved her to another station.

Again she got frustrated, and stayed only an hour and a

half longer. Ed asked if she wanted to help with the computers and she said no. "I'm not coming back. I'm outta here."

Compare her efforts to Ian Yaffe's. Ian first came to the Kitchen a few years ago when he was an eighth-grader at Georgetown Day School. Their eighth-grade class split up and went to different organizations to do community service. Ian started coming once a week with his class (about 13 other kids). Initially, he was like the other students, but he quickly became a standout with his enthusiasm and his work.

He started going to Ed every time he came in. "Hey, Ed, how's it going? What are you doing? I want to help Miss Dorothy today." Or he'd ask about a specific trainee, wanting to work with him or her.

Ian loved the people and became attached to the trainees. He chose to come both semesters and was down here all the time. When school was about to end, he kept telling Ed he wanted to continue volunteering in the summer. Yeah, right, Ed thought. A kid his age is going to get out of school and this kitchen is going to be the last place he'll want to be over the summer.

Ian's family went on summer vacation, but as soon as he returned he called Ed and started coming back in to volunteer. He would bring friends whenever they had free time. Ian bought his own chef coat and also started up a newsletter at school about the work he and his friends contribute every month and the food science at the Kitchen. In the fall, he organized a fund-raising bake sale, asking people for contributions and raising about $700 for the kitchen. He talks with them about our ethos at the Kitchen—he gets it and passes it along to others. And to think he's only in the 11th grade now.

Whether you're a teenager trying to make a difference or the executive director of a service organization, you have four priorities in "doing good." These priorities feed down from one to the next.

THE FOUR PRIORITIES OF DOING GOOD

CAUSE → CLIENTS → COMMUNITY → CONSTITUENCIES

In every instance, cause should be the number one priority. But here's the catch: You have think of cause in a more global sense. Cause isn't as simple as hunger or homelessness or education. Those are the symptoms. We need to redefine our causes by taking a more holistic approach to these terms. In the homelessness movement, for example, their cause isn't just about building more houses. It includes a host of related issues: It's about getting the tenants to a place in life where they can hold on to their jobs and be responsible tenants; it's about getting the government to provide the necessary legislation and zoning to secure affordable housing; it's about local nonprofit agencies setting up the proper training and support needed to help people make a successful transition to permanent housing. The cause is about creating systems that enable people who were once homeless to get themselves in a position in life where homelessness is no longer a symptom of their other problems.

Cause is necessarily intertwined with the second priority of doing good, your clients. Most decisions you make about your cause are related to how well they serve your clients. So if you're good at addressing your cause, you'll naturally be doing a good job addressing your clients. If I'm in the hunger movement and my food pantry opens only twice a week, I'm not serving my cause, and thus, I am not effectively serving my clients. But the same is not true the other way around. An organization fixated too heavily on its clients will lose sight of what's important within the larger sector. Remember the hunger crusaders that tried to feed every kid enrolled in a D.C. summer program? They're a good example of people who put clients first instead of cause. In fact, as I'll explain later in this chapter, if you reverse any of your priorities, you run the risk of damaging the others.

Similarly, if an organization does its utmost to serve its clients, it will serve its third priority, the community. A social service nonprofit's greatest contribution to the community is to serve its clients. By taking people off the street and giving them jobs, training kitchens like D.C. Central and FareStart in Seattle are doing a tremendous service helping out their communities.

The fourth and final priority in this chain of doing good is also the most controversial. Taking care of constituencies such as staff, board members, individual and corporate donors, and foundation officials eats up an inordinate amount of any nonprofit's resources and time. Yet in this climate of highly competitive funding, a lot of nonprofits are forced to devote themselves to the fourth priority, their donor constituents. And some organizations find themselves in the uncomfortable position of adapting their mission to fit the guidelines of a funder.

"People running the country, or giving out money, and people running foundations develop their own criteria for things they think are sexy. And sometimes because you need money to survive, you follow the money and you end up developing or adding on programs to what you do," said Mimi Silbert of Delancey Street in a published interview several years ago. She noted, as an example, "There's a lot of money for AIDS. So you're a drug program but you now add on a big AIDS population [to attract funding]."

Over the past 30 years, Mimi Silbert has turned Delancey Street, based in San Francisco, into a multimillion-dollar social enterprise that houses 1,500 full-time residents—former felons, drug addicts, and homeless people—who help oversee 20 different businesses around California and the Southwest. The ventures range from an award-winning restaurant to a top-rated moving company, and bring in almost $10 million in revenues every year.

Silbert has never applied for a grant in all the years Delancey Street has been in operation. She'll gladly take donations, if offered, but she doesn't want to be a slave to the grant system. She knows that once you start chasing money, you start to lose sight of your mission.

Or as J. R. Ewing said, "Once you lose your integrity, the rest is a piece of cake."

Another recent trend among nonprofits is to engage in cause-based marketing campaigns with for-profit companies. These relationships can be extremely lucrative. The breast cancer movement has raised hundreds of millions of dollars by hooking up with for-profit companies. In the month of October, breast cancer awareness month, you can "Cook for the Cure" with KitchenAid mixers, "Clean for the Cure" with Eureka vacuum cleaners, "Get Fit for the Cure" with Wacoal bra fitting, "Sip for the Cure" with Republic Tea, and "Charge for the Cure" with American Express. Advocates of this type of cause-based marketing claim it's a win-win relationship, creating "new wealth" for both sides.

I'm all for finding new ways to raise money, but the corporate relationship has to go beyond the quid pro quo of making money for the individual company and the nonprofit. If you're going to get involved in corporate sponsorships and collaborations, remember your first priority—your cause—and try to find ways to serve your cause. It doesn't help anyone but yourself if all you do in these relationships is raise money. Educate the public. Inform it on how you're using the money you raise with a corporate partnership to find long-term solutions to the social problems you're trying to solve. Don't just quote a number or brag about money raised. Give us answers and a plan. If I buy a Eureka vacuum cleaner or a KitchenAid mixer, let me know how that money is being spent to try to put an end to breast cancer. Give me a Web site address that allows me to track where my money goes—which organization or cancer researcher or grassroots group is getting my donation. Again, it's my call to get beyond the "who" and "what" of giving and demanding to know the "how" and "why." Let's get beyond the obvious or simplistic. What does "fighting hunger" or "fighting cancer" really mean? How and why are we addressing these causes? Corporate marketing needs to answer these types of questions if these partnerships are truly win-win for both businesses and nonprofits.

Furthermore, there are unseen costs associated with corporate relationships. Critics have complained that companies such as American Express spend more than what they donate to charities to advertise these same philanthropic efforts. Others have questioned whether it's ethical for an organization to "lease" its cause in order to exploit the goodwill and generosity of the public. What happens, for example, when one of these win-win relationships goes sour, or an organization uses this cause to abuse the trust of the people?

The story of Dan Pallotta and Pallotta TeamWorks provides the best cautionary tale of what happens when your priority is chasing money. Between 1994 and 2002, Pallotta organized nationwide events such as the AIDSRide bicycle trips, Avon 3-Day Walks for Breast Cancer, and the African AIDSTrek. If you live in a large enough city, you're probably familiar with these events because at some point you've been hit up by a friend, co-worker, or relative to donate to one of them.

Participants were required to raise minimum donations (for the last AIDSRide in D.C., the entry fee was $2,400). In exchange, Pallotta's company coordinated the support crew and amenities for the participants. Each trek featured caravans of food, tents, and staff, and at the end of every event was a grand ceremony honoring the participants and the cause.

Over a 10-year period, Pallotta TeamWorks raised more than $222 million for causes such as AIDS and breast cancer. The number looks impressive, until you start scratching the surface. Pallotta TeamWorks collected more than $406 million for these events, which means that only 55 percent of the money raised was going to the cause. People were outraged to learn that Pallotta TeamWorks was charging anywhere from $225,000 to $400,000 per event on top of its corporate' sponsorships that helped pay for marketing and promotion. Dan Pallotta refused to disclose how much money he was personally making from these events. Now, money is cool, and as we say in the biz, "No bucks, no Buck Rogers," but every dollar comes at a price. Let's not rob ourselves of the real currency we need to operate in this sector—trust.

Eventually, the public wised up, and got turned off by the feel-good pomp and circumstance, the constant self-promotion (Pallotta's books and future events were plugged hard during final ceremonies), and the overhyped nature of these events. They wanted more results from their hard fund-raising efforts, and were incensed to hear of the ridiculously high overhead at some of these events. At the 2002 D.C. AIDSRide, for example, 86 cents of every dollar raised was spent on overhead and expenses. In the end, $3.6 million had been collected by riders, but only $500,000 was distributed to local AIDS-related agencies.

What was the net cumulative effect? Pallotta strip-mined the causes of AIDS and breast cancer for his own gain. He was able to enlist 125,000 riders and walkers around the country to raise money for something they *really believed in*, only to have them find out that much of their hard-earned donations were going into his company. The damage to the public's faith and trust in these types of fund-raising events is immeasurable.

What's worse about this, though, is that the AIDS- and breast cancer–related agencies that grew to depend on this flow of money were not only left without that guaranteed revenue stream, but have had to pick up the pieces left behind by Pallotta. They have to contend with an angry and betrayed donor pool, a local community that's more wary of these types of charitable events, and operations that grew accustomed to the cash flow from these events.

Pallotta's company folded in 2002, but its impact on the sector lingers to this day. It's a painful reminder that the next time you donate time or money to an organization, agree to raise money for a cause, or decide to steer your organization in a strategic direction, ask yourself the simple question, Whom am I serving? You might be surprised by the clarity and insight you get.

CHAPTER 6

M=EC²

If you're a leader but no one's following you, you're just taking a walk.

— BEECHER HICKS, minister, Metropolitan
Baptist Church

Foundation overlords, philanthropists, and nonprofit leaders love their lingo. Over the last 10 years buzzwords like "measurable impact," "capacity," "efficiency," and "transparency" have gained increasing currency even though these words have such broad meanings that they lose any applicable value. How do you judge the "impact" of, say, a teen health center? You can't measure how many girls *didn't* get pregnant. Or how do you measure the "efficiency" or "performance" of a global nonprofit? By looking at its 990 tax return? *Puh-leeze.* The same creative accounting methods that brought us Enron and the dot-com bust are used by the nonprofit sector.

Every program sets its own parameters to measure these buzzwords. In a study by the Brookings Institution, 250 non-profit leaders around the nation were asked to define "organizational effectiveness," one of the hot terms in the sector. The respondents provided a "range of answers" that revealed little consensus among the group. Less than half of the respondents mentioned the nonprofit's mission as being important to "organizational effectiveness," and just 4 percent talked about good leadership. These words mean something different for everybody.

I'll use one of my own examples to illustrate the point. One of the most common errors people make is to assume that "administrative overhead" is an accurate barometer of an organization's effectiveness. We train people to assume that if a high percentage of every donation goes to serving the "cause," the organization is "efficient." How many events or mailings have you seen in which an organization proudly claims that 80 percent to 100 percent of your donation goes to serving the cause? That's great information, but does that really translate into action or results? Don't forget that the Grate Patrol operation was a classic example of low overhead. One hundred percent of the money went into the program. It was run entirely by volunteers. No one got paid, and the Salvation Army covered the costs of transportation. But what was happening? The volunteers were shopping at Safeway, and at the end of the night, no one was getting off the street. It just goes to show that "efficiency" doesn't translate into "effective."

To put it another way, let's say you're at a gas station and two drivers approach you asking for money. They're both carrying the exact same cargo—their mission—and they're both trying to get to the same destination. As a potential donor, you care about their cause and really want to help one of them as much as possible, but you're not sure which one to help out.

The first driver tells you he'll use 100 percent of your money on gas (how often have you heard this at a fund-raising event?), while the second driver can spend only 75 percent on gas. Which one do you give to? Seems simple, doesn't it? But then you take a look at their vehicles, and see that Driver One is behind the wheel of a giant SUV that gets maybe 15 miles per gallon on a good clear day. Driver Two, meanwhile, has a fuel-efficient hybrid that gets 50 miles per gallon. Now which one would you want to support?

If these factors were all we had to consider, helping out nonprofits would be a breeze. But it's way more complicated than figuring out operating efficiency. You have to consider other factors: Driver One carries a bigger load; Driver Two can use the extra 25 percent on a map and supplies; the list goes on and on, but you get the picture.

The bottom line I'm trying to get you to see is that *there is no bottom line.* No one has been able to come up with a reliable set of metrics or standards to judge nonprofits. The Better Business Bureau probably comes closest to an accurate set of standards, but even its system falls short. Why? Because of the very nature of the nonprofit sector. Nonprofits provide a service, sometimes tangible, sometimes intangible, and it's impossible to create a tool that can accurately measure these services across the board with other agencies. Every nonprofit has its own specific set of conditions that helps determine success or failure in a program.

The job-training class at the Kitchen, for example, has a dropout rate of anywhere between 15 percent and 40 percent of the entering class. These numbers don't look so good on the surface, but when you consider the fact that we're dealing with men and women who've had a 0 percent success rate in life, the 15 percent to 40 percent doesn't look that bad. Plus, we have no way of measuring positive impact our program had on people who didn't graduate. Time and again we've had people drop out of the training program, only to show up a few months later cleaned up and in better shape than before. They'll reenter the program with a powerful sense of determination and then find and hold on to a job after graduation. How do you measure this type of impact? Or how do you transfer this measurement to measure another job-training program?

For decades experts have tried to come up with standards and measurements for the sector. They've offered checklists and evaluation tools, but nothing really sticks. We tell people to watch out for organizations that use a lot of their money on fund-raising or organizational overhead, but any entrepreneur knows you can't run an efficient business without organizational costs. And how about the cost of fund-raising? Most people think the world of Habitat for Humanity, for good reasons. It's one of the best nonprofits in the country when it comes to impact and effectiveness. But did you know that 22 percent of its expenses go to fund-raising, a figure that most people would say is too high for any organization—except Habitat. (Incidentally, Habitat's highest-paid executive makes only $100,000, which is downright modest compared to other nonprofits of comparable size.) It just shows that we can't use any one figure or any one statistic as a barometer for measuring the worthiness of a nonprofit.

A well-run, innovative nonprofit—the kind donors and volunteers love to support—just seems to get it, without trying to fit into any set definitions or parameters. But the one thing these organizations seem to have in common is the fact that they're all resourceful. They get maximum results with the minimum amount of resources.

At the Kitchen we have to be resourceful out of necessity as a food-rescue and kitchen operation. We started out with the motto "Waste is wrong—be it food, money, or the potential for productive lives." We learned to be creative with our concept of efficiency, not because we were smarter than everyone else but because we had to stretch ourselves to make sure the food supplies and the funding would last as long as possible.

So with that in mind, when a restaurant donates 200 pounds of chicken and 50 cans of tomato sauce, you make chicken parmesan, right? Wrong. You chop the chicken into cubes, go into our pantry, and throw in chickpeas, carrots, and leftover potatoes to make chicken chili. You not only feed 10 times as many people, but you're offering food that is packed with nutritional content.

Some people would stop there. We can't afford to. We know that once we think out of the box, we're just in an even bigger box. We constantly have to figure out ways to achieve maximum impact using food as a tool—impact meaning the nourishment of the food itself, its ability to empower the individuals who make it, and the publicity and community goodwill that can be generated by such efforts. For example, let's say you get the chicken and tomato donation in January. You make your chicken chili but you hold a contest among the trainees to boost their confidence as budding chefs. You invite the mayor, local chefs, and donors to serve as judges. Have the community newspaper post the winning recipe in its Sunday food section, just in time for the Super Bowl, and post the recipe on your Web site.

Resourcefulness means getting the steak *and* the sizzle—every last piece of it cut up to serve 50. It means using "everything but the oink" to feed and empower people, but then finding a way to use even the oink to get people's attention.

Change is constant in the nonprofit world. Populations shift, problems mutate like viruses. A nonprofit has to go with the flow, constantly adapting its mission to meet the needs of the cause and the clients, constantly pushing the organization, the employees, and the constituents to be able to adjust to these changes. Every step of the way, an organization has to think about being more resourceful.

The good news is that most of everything we need is right in front of us. It's as if we've been using the equation $M=EC^2$ for the past 100 years to create change in society. We've been frustrated with the results, but rather than question the basic equation, we call for radical new changes. We want privatization in the sector and a more businesslike approach to our problem solving. But rather than look for new answers, we have to recognize that the answer is right in front of us. It has been all along, if we can just look to rearrange things and see things more cleverly. $M=EC^2$ becomes $E=MC^2$ and suddenly we have a formula that not only works but turns out to be incredibly powerful.

One of the best examples of a nonprofit using existing resources also happens to be one of the most successful revenue-generating nonprofits in the country. Pioneer Human Services in Seattle, Washington, manufactures and distributes for for-profit companies. It builds cargo liners for Boeing, handles distribution and repackaging duties for Hasbro, and also operates the Mezza Café inside the Seattle headquarters of Starbucks. It employs 1,000 people and has annual revenues exceeding $50 million. If you think these numbers are impressive, wait till you hear the kicker: 75 percent of Pioneer's workforce is made up of former criminals and drug offenders. Pioneer has taken an existing resource, the men and women who've been cast out from society and overlooked in the $M=EC^2$ equation, and converted them into $E=MC^2$ employees.

Less than 1 percent of the organization's funds comes from foundations and philanthropy. The other 99 percent comes from the revenues created by the 12 divisions at Pioneer. Each division averages about 13 percent annual return, numbers that would be the envy of most CEOs and shareholders in the private sector. And because it's a nonprofit, all of the profit gets reinvested into the organization.

"We measure our worth not just in terms of dollars but also in terms of making a difference. How many more lives can we touch if we add more business?" said the president and CEO of Pioneer, Mike Burns, in an interview several years ago.

Pioneer suffers from a high turnover rate, but that's fine with Burns. It means that Pioneer employees are finding better jobs in the private sector. If they didn't have high turnover, Pioneer would not be fulfilling its mission.

Back at the Kitchen, I've been dealing with new issues of resourcefulness, and one of my biggest concerns is the subject I mentioned before: improving on the 10,000-square-foot facility we're in. We got the space free, but with so many years of use, things have begun to fall apart. In fact, all around the country, the first generation of community kitchens we helped open are in desperate need of updating their equipment and space. Many of them, like D.C. Central, are using free space in local churches, shelters, or drug-treatment facilities. Most have been very successful attracting volunteers, food, and trainees, but now they're working in tight quarters with aging equipment. These colleagues and I are also aware of the population shift of aging boomers, and the growing need to find new ways of making and distributing food in our respective communities.

The first impulse is for kitchens around the country to launch capital campaigns that raise anywhere between $50,000 and $4 million to fund these improvements. But then there are ramifications we have to consider, as discussed earlier. Three million dollars out of the community to build a new kitchen means up to $3 million that wouldn't be spent somewhere else for some other cause. We can't be blind to the needs and goals of other nonprofits. We can't isolate our needs from Our Cause.

One day I was thinking over this quandary while I was visiting my parents in Indiana. I was driving along a road asking myself how the kitchens and food banks around the country would be able to improve their position without creating new facilities from the ground up. Where do you find places in every community where good, reliable kitchen space could be rented or borrowed or given to you? Just then I topped a hill and came upon a new high school.

Eureka.

There are 60,000 school-based cafeterias across America. Most are closed by 3:00 p.m. In many of the high schools around the country, students are required to perform community service to graduate. In fact, high school volunteering is at its highest level in 50 years. Fifty-nine percent of all high school students (13.3 million kids) volunteer, at an average of 3.5 hours a week (2.4 billion hours with a value of $7.7 billion).

I've always wondered, Why do we in the service sector expect volunteers to get in a car or on a bus to schlep across town just to do a good deed? Why do we make them get in a car, drive to a community kitchen or food bank, work for a few hours, and then drive back home? Isn't there a better way to instill the idea of public service where *they* live, work, and play?

Service organizations should make the volunteer process as easy as possible, and as fulfilling as possible. Here in front of me was a fantastic resource—fresh kid brains, all full of interest, vigor, and youth—yet it's never dawned on us in the nonprofit sector to go to *them*. Again, like the working mother who needs to get food assistance, we make volunteers fit into *our* schedule, *our* system, *our* routine, rather than think outside that box and provide services that make it easier for them to give.

If many high schools require their seniors to serve certain community service hours before graduating, why not put community kitchens in these school kitchens and have the students volunteer on-site after classes are over? It also follows that our universities are now, in fact, brimming with kids who've been raised to do community service. Only now they're prebusiness or premed. They're learning about business management skills, journalism, early childhood development, education, and nutrition. They're continuing their desire to give as they learn a valuable profession. And hopefully some day they will be able to share some of their giving not by quitting their lucrative job and trying to find a nonprofit career that gives them more meaning, but by applying the true meaning of giving to whatever career they're in. We don't need to produce more followers to fit into the multimillion-person payroll of the nonprofit sector. We need to produce more leaders in other areas of our economy—leaders with a social conscience and a mission to do good and do it smart in whatever they do. The Campus Kitchen, in this sense, would be an exciting hands-on classroom that could teach the life skills of giving to young volunteers.

In September 2001, D.C. Central Kitchen launched the Campus Kitchen Project, its first official campus kitchen, on the grounds of St. Louis University. With a large grant from founding partner Sodexho, the Campus Kitchen Project partners with the major student-run service organizations and corporate food service programs at each school. The service organizations help enlist energetic volunteers and also researches where to send the meals in the local community, while the food service department donates recyclable food, provides kitchen space, and oversees all safety procedures. At a time when few models can get up to scale beyond their home communities, we've come up with a business model that works anywhere there's a school. All that's needed for now is an initial investment of $50,000 and the consent of the school and food program. Everything else is there . . . and always was there: the volunteers, the space, the food, and the willingness.

The pilot program at St. Louis started with 360 student volunteers. They make about 2,200 meals a month, mainly on Sundays, when the kitchen facilities are closed. Some students cook, some deliver.

Karen Borchert, the cofounder and director of the project, set up the program so that volunteers not only make meals, but also hand deliver them to their recipients. Mentors who tutor young kids in the community work in the kitchen and then take a meal with them. Volunteers who work with seniors help out the Meals on Wheels program by delivering to individual homes and senior centers. On Valentine's Day, the student volunteers even make homemade Valentine cards for every senior they serve, and they hand them out at various locations around St. Louis.

The St. Louis Campus Kitchen also delivers food to the Salvation Army and local homeless shelters. Karen has set up a partnership with Habitat for Humanity to provide first home meals for people who've just moved into a new house.

"We could open a community kitchen anywhere," says Karen. "The fact that we're opening at a college kitchen is our special focus—college students. We're about providing a leadership-development program."

Through Campus Kitchens, students see that service opportunities don't require traveling to the "other side of town." They can be found in your own backyard. And by working with both younger kids and seniors, they see the link between food and health, one reason why the USDA also funds the high school version of the Campus Kitchen Project through the American School Food Service Association (ASFSA), which runs kitchens in Lawrence, Massachusetts; Miami, Florida; Albuquerque, New Mexico; and Savannah, Georgia.

See where we're going? The Campus Kitchen Project has expanded to Dillard University in New Orleans and Northwestern University in Illinois. Karen is overseeing the opening of three more programs, at Marquette University in Milwaukee, Loyola College in Baltimore, and Augsburg College in Minneapolis. And thanks to great pro bono work from the law firm Shaw Pittman, we've been able to provide safety and sanitation insurance policies at every school. We're not going to be satisfied until there are hundreds of Campus Kitchens across the nation.

Like the Central Kitchen, the Campus Kitchen Project is a true model program. The kitchens use resources that exist in every community. And they teach people in those communities to see and use these resources with a greater sense of purpose. They see themselves and their role in the community differently. Like our volunteer Ian Yaffe, they *get* it.

"We talk about creating a new generation of service-minded professionals," Karen says. "We don't want the students to think that the future is starting more nonprofits, or to see the world in boxes where I go to school in one place, work in another, and do good deeds somewhere else. We want them to see how they're all connected. We want them to bring service into their professional life, as part of their life. We want them to understand that the future isn't in nonprofits acting more like businesses, but for businesses to act more like nonprofits."

And that's what it's all about. . . .

As students of charity, whether we're young or old, we need to understand that the best thing we can do to help a child in need is not to give that child another meal or tutor, but to pay that child's parents a living wage. We need to stop thinking we have to drive to the "other side of town" to help "inner-city kids," or go out at night serving meals on the street. That's addressing the symptom, not the disease of poverty. We need to look at the people right next to us to see how they need our help. One hundred years after Carnegie, we're still treating the patient, not cleaning out the cesspool that caused the illness.

This realization came to me during the Internet boom, when dot-com millionaires began approaching us trying to expand their philanthropic efforts. God bless them, they rolled up their sleeves and worked. They cooked at the Kitchen, they cleaned up rivers and neighborhoods, they sponsored hundreds of great programs, and they really strove to close the "digital divide" by providing computers and tutoring "needy" kids in low-income communities.

But then an interesting thing happened. One of our training-program graduates was offered an interview for a job at the employee cafeteria at AOL in its headquarters in Dulles, Virginia. She was sooooo excited. You'd think that she was going to be piloting a spaceship the way she carried on. Everyone thought her hiring signaled a great new era in partnership between D.C. Central Kitchen and AOL. Imagine the headline: "Yep, we're partnering with media giant AOL to get folks jobs."

Then I found out how much she was being offered: $8 an hour for a job that required her to commute nearly 30 miles each way from downtown D.C. That's when the folly of modern philanthropy and our nonprofit game plan really became apparent. So much of nonprofit work was about cleaning up somebody else's yard. The reality is that we need to clean up our own backyards and take care of our own communities.

Imagine how wild it would be for an AOL executive who drives into D.C. to tutor an inner-city kid, who feels sorry for the kid because she doesn't have basic necessities like food and clothing, to learn that the kid's parent works every day in the AOL cafeteria and doesn't make enough to take proper care of herself and her child.

Sweet irony, huh?

The point is, we don't have to look far to find ways to make a difference. Instead of crossing the train track to "do good," fix the problems at home. Pay your employees more than $8 an hour. Mentor young leaders in your office or be a big brother or sister to children in *your* neighborhood. Motivate your co-workers to get the corporate cafeteria to sponsor a Meals on Wheels program, or organize a monthly outing for your department to volunteer at a local food bank or community kitchen.

Community kitchens and Pioneer Human Services show us that you don't have to buy new or pay big bucks to someone from the outside to get results. Be resourceful in every way, including in the people you're working with. Focus on *your* community, *your* city, *your* neighbors, *your* brothers and sisters. The answer to our problem, as Dorothy found out in *The Wizard of Oz,* has been with us all along. All it takes is for you to start seeing things differently. Before you know it, $M=EC^2$ becomes $E=MC^2$. Magic? No. Resourcefulness? You bet.

CHAPTER 7

The Tangible Link

The only difference between a derelict and a man is a job.
— GODFREY SMITH in *My Man Godfrey*,
1936

What do you teach people who've had a lifetime of addiction, failure, adversity, or poverty to get him or her on a path toward self-sufficiency? How do you create positive, lasting change? We had to answer this question as we designed the training program at the Kitchen.

Your answer might be knowledge because everyone knows that knowledge is power. It's true that the training program teaches students how to clean and prep food, how to dice and chop, and how to make everything from a roasted turkey to a ratatouille, safely. At the end of their 12-week program, the trainees get a diploma—in many cases the first diploma they've ever received—along with a food handler's certificate that allows them to get a job in just about any kitchen in the country.

Yet all of this knowledge is worthless unless it can be leveraged into something bigger and better. Something permanent. There isn't a cookbook, classroom, or instructor that can force the graduates to get up on time every day, stay clean and off the streets, and then stick to a job until they get a raise and move up the socioeconomic ladder. They have to want to do it themselves and learn how to do it on their own.

But how do you instill that desire? You have to use what I call the tangible link, and then create lasting change with what I call the calculated epiphany.

When we started the job-training program, we knew the trainees would never get anywhere if they didn't learn and discover the process on their own. We wouldn't be able to elicit the same feelings of pride, accomplishment, and confidence that are the required building blocks for individual success. The trainees have to *want* it, and no "cabin in the sky" promises of better things down the road will get them there.

With these ideas in mind, we set out to design the training program as something in between regular school and a vocational class. Trainees arrive no later than 9:00 a.m. and cook with volunteers until noon. They help load the trays of food they've just cooked into our delivery vans, then take a lunch break. From 2:00 p.m. to 3:00 p.m. they take a culinary or life skills class. Each day they learn to interact with people of various backgrounds. They build values such as accountability, time management, and financial responsibility, often for the first time in their lives.

We were conscious about treating the trainees as adults, not sympathy cases, and we were especially mindful not to use language that referred to "them" or "us." If we were going to make it as an organization, we'd have to get away from the disconnect that this type of language creates. We were in this together, and we weren't about to propagate any stereotypes about who was helping and who was needy.

We also let the trainees know from day one that they control the power to decide their own fate. At the beginning of every training session, I tell the entering class, "I'm not here to be your friend. I'm here to give you an opportunity that you can take or leave. The decision is up to you." The trainees learn they have the choice, and the power, to make it through the program if they choose to. We put everything in place for them to succeed or fail. It's up to them.

This ain't about bromides, but a blueprint. This is about short steps we take every day that lead up the mountain to that vantage point from which we can all see the other side.

We have always enjoyed the view. They know that if they arrive at the Kitchen late, if they fail one drug test, if they don't pass the skills test at the end of the program, they don't get to strut down the aisle to the tune of "Brand New Day," by Bill Withers, for their graduation ceremony. We also remind them that if they decide not to show up on any given day, the meals won't get made and sent out to our partner agencies. We're not giving them a guilt trip; it's just a simple fact. We run a business of feeding people, and as part of this system, they have an obligation to show up and work hard.

I also tell the trainees on the first day of every class, "Today you'll help someone you'll never meet, and because of your work, they'll begin a journey that may, one day, lead them to this door, where they'll join the class and start the process all over again." At the Kitchen, everyone's a giver, and giving is one of the keys.

Training classes average between 10 and 20 students. During the first few days, we'll get a few dropouts. Sometimes the numbers are as high as 25 percent of the entering class. Over time we'll lose a few more for a variety of reasons. It's not an easy path for anyone, but that's why it's all the more rewarding for the ones who make it. Just because some of these trainees have been down a rough road, we can't turn this boot camp into a day camp. That wouldn't be showing respect, and in turn that wouldn't be generating respect.

Our first class of trainees enrolled on Martin Luther King's birthday, January 20, 1990, a year after Bush Sr.'s inauguration. The program had 10 trainees, referred to us by social workers, drug counselors, and parole officers in the D.C. area. Nobody had a clear idea how the program would work, but we had a general sense of what we wanted to accomplish and made our way in that direction. Each day brought a valuable new lesson. Some of our methods worked well, while others completely flopped. And then there were a few that were so eye-openingly transformational that they helped us move along in perfecting the program.

One of these moments took place during our first class of trainees. Reggie was one of these students, a slender black man in his early 30s who had been battling a heroin addiction. Reggie had been clean for about 90 days and had been referred to us by a local drug-treatment center.

Everything in the world said Reggie would flunk our training program and fall back into his habits and onto the streets. He had no close family members or relatives to watch his back. But he had plenty of other "friends" who wanted nothing more than to see Reggie fail. Like many people in Reggie's position, there was a destructive voice in his head that constantly questioned his abilities: *Who the hell do you think you are? You can't do this! You're just a washed-out dope user with an eighth-grade education. Why even try? You're just going to fuck up like you've done with everything else in your life.*

Despite the odds, Reggie hung on during these early days of the program, returning day after day, on time and ready to work. Then one morning a group of medical doctors came into the kitchen to volunteer. They were white, middle-aged men who'd made a pact a long time ago to serve the community once a month. On this particular month, they'd decided to volunteer at the Kitchen, and when they arrived I asked Reggie to guide these volunteers through the morning routine.

Reggie didn't respond. His body stiffened, as did those of the middle-aged doctors. *You want me to work with them?* he seemed to be saying to me.

I turned to the doctors and saw a similar look on their faces. *You want us to work with him?*

I could feel an invisible barrier rising up between Reggie and the group. Everyone was hiding behind a mask to shield his discomfort. Not knowing what else to do, I told Reggie to hurry up and get the doctors started, and walked away wondering if I'd made a big mistake.

Twenty minutes later I came back to a beautiful scene. Reggie was standing in the middle of the group showing the doctors how to julienne carrots. Reggie knew how to do something the doctors didn't, and that fact seemed to make all the difference. The tension had disappeared. The dynamics in the group had shifted. Reggie now spoke with confidence, and the doctors stood side by side with him listening attentively.

They asked Reggie questions about his life. He told them about his struggle with heroin, about his three little girls who lived with their mother in "PG," Prince George's County, and about his dream of working in the kitchen of one of the black-owned restaurants downtown. The doctors were taking it all in, quiet, but visibly engaged and impressed.

Hot damn! I thought. This is how we'll do it from now on. We'll bring in every volunteer in a three-state radius—every kid, every spring breaker, every retiree, every corporate volunteer we can lay our hands on—and we'll put the trainees in charge of the whole shooting match. We'll have these two groups interacting together with the common purpose of making meals.

The idea brought me back to plans of my nightclub. After seeing so many shows in my life, I was tired of going to clubs and concerts and standing in the center of the floor looking up at the performers. Somehow, live performance had become routine. We accepted this almost Pavlovian ritual—the preshow chatter, the lights go down, and we all turn to the stage and watch the performance. We whoop, we listen, we applaud, we hold up our lighters, we leave. I wanted to break the physical and mental barriers between the artists and the audience. My club was going to have multiple stages on different parts of the floor. One act would finish just as another would pop up somewhere else. You'd never know where it was coming from or what would happen next. I called it guerrilla showbiz.

When I saw Reggie and his cadre of doctors, I realized that the volunteer experience at the Kitchen should follow the same concept. Break down the walls between the two groups so that each person could see, hear, experience, and learn something from a person he'd never otherwise meet or interact with in his life. You aren't strangers anymore. You're fellow travelers on the same journey.

The tangible link was born.

What is the tangible link? It's the connection between effort and purpose. Practically speaking, it's the bond that nonprofits create between their donors and recipients, workers and customers, and everyone else in between. It's Ben Franklin's old notion of face-to-face giving and empowerment but tied to a larger philanthropic purpose.

Effective nonprofit organizations know (and all should learn) how to cultivate the potential tangible links between their constituencies. Habitat for Humanity is probably the most successful and recognized organization that does this well. Habitat volunteers work alongside family members whose houses they're helping build. Driving a nail into a two-by-four becomes more fun than hard work when you have a tangible link with the recipient of your good deed. Like the group of doctors who met Reggie at the Kitchen, people who volunteer at Habitat walk away from a housing site changed in some way. As walls of each Habitat house go up, the invisible walls of stereotypes and false impressions get torn down.

Another inspiring example of the tangible link comes from Gainesville, Florida, with an organization called the Dignity Project. Founded in 1998 by Todd Livingston, the Dignity Project teaches high school students who have dropped out or are at risk of dropping out of school the basics of car repair. With the help of one full-time mechanic and a full-time helper, he enrolls kids into either an after-school program or a full-time auto academy. Most of these young men have a history of problems at home or at school, but through the Dignity Project, they're given newfound structure and meaning in their lives. That's because these students are not only learning about auto repair, they're learning about giving: Every donated car they fix is then handed over to a low-income family in the Gainesville area.

Like the trainees at the D.C. Central Kitchen, many of Todd's students are learning how to be responsible for the first time in their lives. "We try to teach the kids the world doesn't owe them anything—that if they want something they've got to do it on their own," Todd says.

Todd also teaches them that they can make money and at the same time they can do good for their community. In the first year of the program Todd and the kids fixed 17 cars. This year, with a dozen students in the academy and 35 students in the after-school program, they're on pace to fix up more than 120. Todd now gets a car donated nearly every day of the week. The ones in great shape—valued at $7,500 and up—are sold in the market to keep the Dignity Project running. The cars on the low end that can't run will be stripped for parts for a few hundred bucks. All other cars in between will be fixed up by the students and handed over to someone in need.

Where is the tangible link? It happens every time a new client comes to pick up a car. Todd has structured these pickups as a celebration for the new car owner. All of the kids in the program wait beside the new car for the person to arrive. After greeting the owner, they give the person a tour of the vehicle, pointing out any quirks or special features of the particular model. They also show the owner how to perform basic maintenance tasks, such as checking the oil and tire pressure.

The cars have an average street value of $2,500, but to the individuals who receive them, they're priceless. A car allows each of the owners—oftentimes men and women who have graduated from programs like the Kitchen and have just landed their first jobs—to commute to their jobs on time, pick up their kids from day care, go to the grocery store or the food bank or the pharmacy before closing. Each vehicle comes with a six-month warranty and guaranteed repairs for the rest of the car's life. The garage does about 500 repairs a year, but Todd doesn't mind the high number, because it's a great way for the students to maintain their link with the car owners.

For many of these kids, the Dignity Project is the first chance they've had to be on the giving end of an exchange. And it feels good. "The kids really care about the families who get these cars," Todd explains. "You can see it on their faces when a person comes back for a repair. It's like a family."

I see this same reaction every day at the Kitchen between our regular volunteers and trainees. One of my favorite regulars is a group of wives from the Chinese embassy who volunteer once a month. As soon as they walk into the Kitchen, their faces light up at the sight of Miss Dorothy. Miss Dorothy gives each of them a hug and a kiss, and then they catch up briefly before getting to work.

Another volunteer, Kate, a recent George Washington University graduate, comes in every two or three weeks at the Kitchen. During one of our training sessions, she developed a good bond with a short trainee named Stovetop (a name given to him because he loves Stove Top stuffing).

"Stovetop!" she'd call out whenever she'd walk in the Kitchen.

"Hey, Shorty," he'd say with a big grin. It was an inside joke. Kate is a blond Caucasian who stands about six feet tall. Stovetop told her their first day working together that he was horrible at remembering names, so he thought it best if he called her "Shorty." Every time Kate came in, Stovetop would give her a good slap on the back and say, "Doing good, Shorty? All right!"

Over time we also learned to create new tangible links that tailored to special events and holidays during the year. During one Passover, we invited students from Edmund Burke Middle School in D.C. to work together with trainees and a local culinary legend, Mel Krupin, to build the world's biggest matzo ball (18 inches in diameter). During African American history month, instead of cooking the usual corn bread and greens, we held a class in which grade-school students and trainees met with the best African American chefs in town to learn about the history and use of African-based ingredients such as sorghum and chicory. We've done this for Cinco de Mayo, St. Patrick's Day, and even anniversaries.

Last year the trainees teamed up with Steve Klc, the pastry

chef at one of the finest restaurants in D.C., Zaytinya, to make a 200-pound cake replica of the Globe Theater, complete with a thatched roof made of shredded wheat. It was for a celebration of Shakespeare's 439th birthday at the Folger Shakespeare Library. More impressive than the baking of the cake was the fact that many of the 850 guests who attended the celebration were able to interact with the D.C. Central trainees who stood by the cake as it was being served. Not only did the trainees get a tangible link with a great talent like Steve, but the guests at the Folger Library event found a tangible link while talking with the trainees.

Volunteers and trainees create lasting impressions about people they might not otherwise meet in their lives. And because they're taking part in a common endeavor, they have an automatic reason to talk and interact with one another. That's a big reason why an organization like Habitat, the Kitchen, or the Dignity Project can be such a powerful learning tool for every side. Whether it's a garage, a house, or a kitchen, these environments act as melting pots where people mix together. They're doing more than building cars or houses. They're building good ideas. They're developing community and communication.

Once we figured out the tangible link, we began asking ourselves the next logical question: How do you get someone to think differently, act differently, and most important, keep that mind-set for as long as possible?

You get them to think like the Greeks. . . .

CHAPTER 8

Taking Troy

What we have here is a failure to communicate.
—CAPTAIN, *Cool Hand Luke,* 1967

I'm interested in two kinds of change: the kind you put in the bank, and the kind you put in people's heads.

The second kind is always harder to get than the first because, frankly, anybody can make money, but not everyone can get people to think differently or accept new ideas. You have to get inside the head of the person you're trying to convince, and that's no easy task. An old friend Joe, a homeless man who has been plagued by voices in his head for the last 20 years, always says when we try to get him to seek help, "Can't do it, won't do it. . . . Can't do it, won't do it."

People have gotten much smarter when someone's trying to sell them on a new idea. In this media-saturated era, we've learned to defend against all types of full-frontal assaults advocating social policy or politics. Everyone from homeless and hunger advocates to presidential candidates tries to pound messages into people's heads using scare tactics and fancy numbers. But the truth is, the public has wised up. It knows a sound bite from a solution. It knows a hard sell from an honest pitch. It also knows the difference between someone who cries wolf and someone who knows how to kill the wolf.

Let me tell you about a recent hunger campaign sponsored by the Ad Council and America's Second Harvest to support this point. For those of you who don't know, the Ad Council produces public service announcements and A2H is the nation's largest food-bank network, with over 200 food banks and food-rescue programs around the country.

The ads are based on a real-life decision many people have to make in their lives: Do I buy food or use the money for another basic necessity such as medicine, gas, child care, or the utility bill? Sounds pretty basic, right? It's the kind of tough decision no person, young or old, should have to make, yet hundreds of thousands of people are confronted with this dilemma every day of their lives.

The premise of the ad campaign is sound, but what I question is its delivery. In one of the print ads, half of the space is taken up by a picture of a blue-eyed, red-haired little girl who's staring sullenly into the camera. The caption above her reads:

Julie is cold. She has chicken skin, she says. She woke up in the middle of the night shivering because I turned the heat down. I'm afraid if my bill gets too high I won't have any money left for food. I pull Julie close and hug her tight. She says she will be fine—she knows she's not really a chicken.

Then below the picture is a line that reads, "Heat or food? 1 in 5 in America faces hunger because of decisions like this."

Wow. That's bad news. Makes you think, doesn't it?

But what do you think? Too bad? Tough choice? There but for the grace of God go I? Does it make you want to know what the plan is? Doesn't it make you want to ask, "Okay, that's a problem, but NOW WHAT?"

Nonprofits have to come to terms with the fact that we can't change someone's mind by quoting a statistic or wagging a moral finger. More important, they have to understand that the public already knows there's a problem; now it needs to know the solution.

We can't continue to propagate a caste system of needy people in which children are at the top because that implies there's someone at the bottom, and it's usually the "Big Uglies": drug addicts, convicts, and homeless people. Let's face it. We've been beating the same save-the-children drum for a hundred years, but in particular since the Kennedy and Johnson administrations. Well, guess what? Some of those children who weren't saved in the '60s and '70s are the homeless people and drug addicts today. And we need to help them just as much as we need to help today's children.

Ads like this one that try to play the pity card are full-frontal assaults on the mind. They're designed to inspire semi-annual contributions, not engineer social change. They're a setback for the rest of us in the nonprofit sector who want to run forward-thinking marketing campaigns that appeal to reason not emotion.

The public is smart. We know there's a hunger problem. We're aware that kids are going hungry every day, just as we know there are issues of racism, drug addiction, stereotypes that plague the country. We already feel awful, so we don't need to be reminded of them. But we've been down this road before. We've seen our money and the government's money being thrown in every possible direction, but we haven't seen any evidence of long-term effective change.

As we said earlier, the public no longer needs to know the who and what of giving. We need to know the how and why. People are hungry? So what? Oh, you have a plan to end hunger? Hallelujah! Let's hear it.

If you want to change someone's attitude, you can't run the same pity campaign nonprofits have been running for years and years. You have to get inside a person's head, infiltrate the defenses, and plant the device to blow up a person's old ideas and insert new ones.

You have to think like the Greeks.

Most of you already know the story of the Trojan horse. The Greeks laid siege to Troy, but Troy's defenses were simply too strong. After 10 years of fighting, the Greek warrior Odysseus came up with an idea to build a giant wooden horse, fill it with his best soldiers, and leave it as a gift. The Trojans brought the horse into the city, and suddenly the war was over.

What I love about this tale is that the Trojans were responsible for their own fate. *Oh look, honey! Someone left us a gift. Let's bring it inside!*

The same approach has to be taken in the war of ideas. You can't get into someone's head to change his or her ideas of hunger or homelessness unless the person lets you in.

I call it the calculated epiphany. Figure out what kind of point you're trying to make, dress it up to look pretty, ring the doorbell, and then run! If you've done everything right, the person will invite your idea inside his head. Once inside, it'll do its work. The rest is easy.

Let's go back to that Second Harvest ad. Imagine if, after getting a person's attention with the picture of the girl, the copy said something like this:

> Everyday, Second Harvest Food Banks save empowerment programs across this country tens of millions of dollars so that they can focus on job training, literacy classes, and after-school programs so that families like this can live independently.
>
> Second Harvest—Using Food as a Tool to Combat Hunger and Build Communities, one family at a time.

People who see the picture of the little girl will think they're going to be scolded or made to feel guilty by nonprofit saints, but instead they get something bold and ambitious. They are informed about the connection between donating money to Second Harvest and getting actual results in the fight against hunger. The message treats them as intelligent partners in the cause, not as suckers expected to open up their wallets without any questions.

People who read this new message will hear the faint sound of wheels turning inside their heads—the sound of their gates opening. They'll think about ways Second Harvest is providing tangible solutions to the hunger issue by freeing up the resources of other agencies. They'll see that food is more than fuel for the body. Things will start to gel in people's heads, creating a chain reaction of new ideas and possibilities. At the very least, people will start to see a way out or an end to what this girl and others in her dilemma are going through—not just temporary relief.

We have a for-profit catering division at the Central Kitchen called Fresh Start that became a test model for the calculated epiphany. Back when the Kitchen was growing into a full-time operation in the early 1990s, we began getting more and more requests for catered events. Small nonprofits or local groups who wanted to raise dough for their efforts kept calling and asking if we would give food in support of their special events. We were looking for something that would help the grads make the next step, and seeing a niche open up, we began to consider opening some sort of catering-employment program. After a little investigating, we discovered that most local catering companies were being overwhelmed with requests from local nonprofits for free or low-cost service. Not wanting to shag business from the very companies that had been so generous to us when we started, we approached some of our best supporters and asked if they would be miffed if we opened a catering company designed to offer reasonably priced support to the local nonprofits. Quite the contrary, they suggested, this was a market they'd love to see someone take on, which is how Fresh Start Catering was born.

Opened in 1995, Fresh Start hires graduates from the D.C. Central Kitchen training program, purchases fresh ingredients, and has catered everything from black-tie galas to open-air festivals on the Washington Mall.

So where's the calculated epiphany? It comes at the end of an event, after everyone's been served good food and conversation. That's when I pop out from behind the curtain or door to speak briefly about the group that just catered their gathering.

"Ladies and gentlemen, I want to thank you for coming out tonight. I want to bring out a very special group of people who helped make this evening possible." I'll wave for the staff of Fresh Start to come out from the kitchen station and line up in front of the audience for applause, just as a cast would at the end of a show.

"These men and women are all graduates of the D.C. Central Kitchen training program. They made all the food you ate tonight and served you as well. . . . Can you give them a round of applause for all their hard work?"

You should see the look on the guests' faces. It's always the same. *You mean the person pouring my coffee was a homeless person and now she has a job through your training program? How cool!* They're visibly excited, and their excitement carries over to the Fresh Start staff, who are all beaming with pride and confidence.

It's like taking candy from a baby while shooting fish in a barrel.

But imagine if I'd popped out before the event started and

said the same thing. I would have received the opposite reaction. The guests would look at the servers with pity or, worse, suspicion, and not as professionals. *You mean this person who's pouring me coffee was homeless? Um . . . how nice. Honey, hold on to your purse and don't touch the food!*

That's what I mean by the calculated epiphany. It's meant to break down the attitudes of people you're serving. I want people to go home saying, "Hey, if former homeless people can cook and serve at a black-tie function, maybe I need to rethink my views." If I told the guests to think that way, I'd be preaching and they wouldn't listen. But if it's *their* idea, then it's their eureka moment, their revelation, their awakening.

In fact, if it's done right, we'll get paid three times per event: once for the event, a second time when we get hired by people who were there and want to drop the same love bomb at their next party, and a third at year's end, when these diners are writing checks to their favorite "charities." We'll be on that list, I guarantee, because these people dig the fact that we're making the effort to make our own scratch.

And while we're doing this, we're fighting hunger on the most important battlefield, the brain.

The same experience happens at the Kitchen, between our volunteers and trainees. The volunteers come into the Kitchen with preconceived notions of their experience. They think of "soup kitchen" and have images in their heads about what they're going to expect serving the poor. We put every new batch of volunteers through a quick orientation about how things work; then we have them wash up, throw on an apron and a hair net, and get to work right away with the trainees. Some of the volunteers don't say much. Others start conversations right away with people next to them. There's always one trainee who's assigned to a station, or squad of volunteers who take their cue from the trainee. He or she shows them how to chop a vegetable properly, how to load and seal a tray of food, or how to judge the meal portions of a serving platter.

If we told the volunteers beforehand that they'd be working alongside former convicts, former drug addicts, and former homeless people, we might not get the 5,000 to 7,000 volunteers coming into the Kitchen every year. A lot of them would be afraid; a lot of them would put up defenses in their minds before they even walked through the door.

But by throwing them right into the fray, you generate a calculated epiphany on either side. You can see their attitude change by the end of the session.

THAT'S how we fight hunger at the Kitchen. By changing people's views, maybe we can get the big-ticket changes further down the road. If we can get young kids, corporate citizens, elected officials to see the logic of what we are doing, then they have to get off the pity bus and hop on the logic train.

I like to set the same trap for politicians and policy makers who come to observe the Kitchen. Two years ago, for example, I had a delegation of senators and congressional reps take a tour. As they stood by watching one of our trainees, Marcel, teach volunteers how to prep food, I told them about Marcel's personal history—that he was a drug addict just months before he came into the training program. Then I told them that Marcel had already landed his first job, at the restaurant in the Thurgood Marshall Building right next to Union Station. He'd start at $10 an hour, but the great thing was that he'd be eligible for a raise after just the first few months. The politicians were elated to hear this news. Here's a guy who was on the street just months before, and not only has he gotten himself cleaned up and off government dependency, he's actually working his butt off to make it on his own. He was once a burden on the system; now he's one of the solutions.

But then I dropped the next logic bomb. "You know, Senator," I said, "Marcel came from a drug-treatment program, Safe Haven, up on North Capitol Street. If we had more support for places like that and fewer jails, we could get more Marcels out there, contributing and paying taxes and being part of society."

I'd be naive to say this exchange changed the senator's views overnight, but at least it opened his mind long enough for this Trojan horse to slip in.

The calculated epiphany is the future of any real advocacy. The realm of social and political debate has become too antagonistic to take a frontal approach to changing people's attitudes. Too often we hear the message from the left that Republicans are evil, or from the right that Democrats are dumb. We hear social advocates blaming society for the problems of individuals, while their opponents blame the individual for not exercising free will or personal responsibility. If we want to see results from advocacy, we need to step away from the blame game and start showing people ways to expose the fallacies and stereotypes in their own thinking.

So if you're trying to advocate for change of any type, no matter what side you're on, don't try to blast through the front door. That approach has been tried for years, and it doesn't work. The issues get tied into personal egos and saving face, which is why so much advocacy gets heated and personal.

We have to turn to new tactics, to guile and finesse, cunning ideas and covert methods. Change requires establishing a connection and then creating a calculated epiphany. It requires shifting the perspective from human needs to economic needs.

As I discussed in previous chapters, the resources are there to make change happen. We just have to start thinking and seeing things differently in order to use these resources. So when there's a problem in front of us, we shouldn't take the attitude of trying to see either the forest or the trees. For 10 years the Greeks used the woods around Troy to build weapons and maintain their camps. They did the obvious.

We need to look at our problems and solutions in a different light. Only Odysseus was clever enough to look out at the woods and see a third thing, a Trojan horse, a tool for ending the war.

CHAPTER 9

Take It to 11

> I will build a motor car for the great multitude. It will be
> large enough for the family but small enough for the
> individual to run and care for. It will be constructed of
> the best materials, by the best men to be hired, after the
> simplest designs that modern engineering can devise. But
> it will be priced so that no man making a good salary will
> be unable to afford one—and enjoy with his family the
> blessings of hours of pleasure in God's open spaces.
>
> —HENRY FORD, introducing the Model T
>   in 1909

Okay, because I'm a history buff, a little more
history . . . When Henry Ford announced to
the world that he would raise the average wage of his factory

workers from $2.34 to $5.00, critics and colleagues alike thought he had lost his mind. Such a move was unheard of in the business world. The Dodge brothers, investors in Ford's company, went so far as to sue him for failing to meet the expectations of his dividend holders. In court proceedings, the Dodges' attorney asked Ford incredulously how it was possible for him to raise wages, lower the price of his cars, *and* still hope to make a profit. No one had done it before.

Ford had the answer, but he knew he'd have to make it happen to prove it to his skeptics. And prove it he did. From 1910 to 1924, he reduced the price of the Model T from $950—or 22 months' worth of wages—to $290—roughly three months of wages. The public loved the car because it was easy to drive, easy to fix, and reliable, thanks to quality control by his well-paid workers. At its peak production, half of all the cars around the world were Tin Lizzies. Ford became a billionaire, and in the 1920s in a survey conducted among American college students, Ford was voted the third greatest figure in history, behind Jesus and Napoleon.

Ford had the audacity to build the world's largest car company because he saw opportunities where others saw barriers. He did whatever was necessary to make a profit, whether it involved paying his employees higher wages or getting thugs to break up unionization efforts in his factories. Like him or not, he knew how to build an empire.

Ray Kroc had a similar ambition. At age 54 he mortgaged his house and bought the rights to a five-spindle blender called the Multimixer. When he heard about two brothers who'd opened a burger joint in California, where the customers walked in and carried out their food instead of being waited on at a table or in their car, Kroc drove to San Bernardino to see the operation for himself.

When he got there, Ray saw a long line of people waiting to order food. Behind the counter were three guys flipping burgers, two workers making fries, and two on the shake machine. Because of the limited menu, customers could get their food fast (an average of 15 seconds per order) and take it with them. Burgers were 15 cents (cheeseburgers were 19 cents), coffee was 5 cents, and, best of all, one-third of the customers were buying the 20-cent milk shakes. The sound of Multimixer sales was ringing like a cash register in Ray's head.

Ray pitched the two brothers, Dick and Maurice McDonald, to expand the franchise. They weren't interested, but agreed to sell Ray the franchising rights. Two years later, Ray had opened 12 McDonald's franchises around the country, and by 1960, he'd opened 228. The rest is history.

You might read these stories of Ford and McDonald's and roll your eyes. Over the years both companies have become for many people symbols of greed, capitalism, and environmental destruction. Yet in their day, Ford and Kroc worked to make life better and easier for all Americans. Ford enabled the average worker to have the freedom of a car. He helped grow America's economy and created thousands of new jobs. His factories' workers earned enough money to afford their own automobiles.

Decades later, Ray Kroc contributed to another important era of American domesticity by offering families a clean, friendly restaurant with reliable service and food. People who were traveling on the road knew they could stop at a McDonald's and get the same quality and service as at any other Mc-

Donald's location. The fast-food conformity we reject today was a godsend for weary travelers back in the '50s and '60s and kids of all generations.

Like Carnegie and Rockefeller before them—and figures like Michael Dell and Bill Gates today—Ford and Kroc knew what their customers wanted. And they had the audacity to try to turn that vision into a reality. They were able to challenge their competitors and see things their critics couldn't. They took chances and succeeded in winning their respective markets.

Unfortunately, it's hard to find the same type of success and ambition in the nonprofit sector. Nonprofits are in the business of "doing good," not making money, and for that reason they don't have the same incentives to think and act big, or to boldly go where no nonprofit has gone before. Entrepreneurs and business-minded people begin any pursuit with the attitude of "How can I make it happen?" In nonprofits, however, you come up against the attitude of "It can't be done" or "We don't have the resources."

Yet every once in a while, you come across pioneers in the sector who constantly push their organizations and always think bigger and better. As the statue of General Patton at West Point reads, these men and women "fight with the utmost audacity." Instead of working for profit, they're creating purpose in what they do. Bernard Glassman is one of these fighters.

When Glassman, a Zen Buddhist priest, decided to open the Greyston Bakery in Yonkers, New York, in the early 1980s, his mission was simple: use the bakery to help individuals in his neighborhood. At the time, Yonkers had the highest per capita rate of homelessness in the country, even though it was located in the highly affluent suburb of Westchester County.

Glassman decided to focus on baking high-ticket items such as cakes and pastries rather than breads and muffins because the profit margins were higher, allowing him to do more with the revenue. Using the Buddhist mandala (circle of life) as his guide for his work, he hired local laborers—many of them homeless or unskilled—and sold the Greyston goods to upscale gourmet shops and restaurants in nearby Manhattan.

Then in 1989 he struck a deal with Ben & Jerry's to be its main supplier of brownies for several lines of ice creams and yogurts. Today Ben & Jerry's accounts for nearly three-quarters of Greyston's $4 million revenues in baked goods every year while also marketing the bakery's actions on the sides of its ice-cream containers.

Glassman kept pushing his ideas to correspond with his mission of serving the people of Yonkers. Recognizing that the needs of the community went beyond his 42-employee bakery, Glassman expanded the scope of his services by creating the Greyston Foundation. In the last 10 years, the Greyston Foundation has successfully developed more than $35 million of real estate projects in Westchester County, and has another $10 million of projects under way, including 176 units of permanent housing for families and single adults.

In addition, the foundation has developed nonresidential projects, including an HIV health care program and a child care center, affordable housing and day care, AIDS treatment, and job opportunities for single mothers. In the spring of 2003, Greyston moved into a new state-of-the-art baking facility that will allow it to expand its social entrepreneurship by increasing production and bringing in more employees.

"What we're trying to do is create a community development model that integrates the for-profit, nonprofit, and spiritual sectors," Glassman said.

Glassman and other nonprofit leaders push the capacity of their organizations. They're constantly expanding their services and always thinking of innovative ways to keep improving on their mission. These are the dividends they chase. No matter how fast or slow, they have the audacity to get the most out of themselves and those around them—and to show the way for other organizations. Audacity means being able to push yourself and those around you to go further than you thought you could go.

And it means "taking it to 11."

You might remember the line from the movie *This Is Spinal Tap*. Back in the early '80s, the crooner Mel Tormé was performing at Charlie's for a weeklong gig. He went to see the movie one afternoon and loved it so much he invited everyone at the club—even the Somalian busboys—to see it with him.

I thought Mel was going to pass out from hysteria during the scene in which the rock star Nils, played by Christopher Guest, shows the documentarian his guitar amp that goes to 11.

Most amps go up only to 10, he explains, but where do you go from there? Nowhere! Sometimes you need that extra push over 10.

"Why not just make 10 louder?"

Nils chews his gum, cigarette in his hand, and stares blankly at the amp. Finally he repeats, "These go to 11."

Nonprofit directors who don't try to take their organization to 11 should pass the torch to someone who can. Unfortunately, the larger or older the organization gets, the harder it becomes to push it in new ways. The priority at these organiza-

ROBERT EGGER
with Howard Yoon

138

tions becomes keeping the machine alive instead of finding innovative ways to improve the machine. This has always been true in the for-profit world, and it applies equally to nonprofits. Henry Ford, for example, showed his genius by producing the Model T, but years later he relied too heavily on the Model T instead of developing a newer model. McDonald's also has suffered recently from its stagnant business practices. Its critics have accused the company of failing to recognize the changing eating habits of consumers, and being too slow to adopt a more health-conscious menu.

These companies, as well as larger nonprofit organizations such as the United Way, have so much at stake in keeping the machine alive that their leaders seldom risk going in new directions. Yet, they have to keep gambling if they are to have any hope of getting new rewards. They have to shake up their organizations, and through their programs let the public see them sweat. They have to prove they're still working hard and pushing themselves.

We want people like Bernie Glassman who'll think out of the box, and then think out of that bigger box, and so on, and so on. We want that leap of faith where the faithful keep leaping.

A few years ago I was at a gathering for the National Restaurant Association when an executive from McDonald's approached me. He was wondering how his company could contribute to America's Promise, an effort headed by Colin Powell to channel the resources of the country to help change "welfare as we know it."

What a perfect question, I told him, because I had just been thinking about this dilemma. "If I were you," I said, "I would structure a campaign to say something like: McDonald's applauds welfare to work because we believe the best thing for America is a solid workforce. We believe our company can offer many people coming off welfare a perfect first job. But we also know that the majority of those coming into the workforce are single moms. Therefore, we are going to add 10 cents onto the price of our Big Mac, and with those dimes we'll develop a national network of child care centers so that those mothers can work and begin to build the kind of skills they'll need to move up the job line and eventually become independent."

The executive looked at me as if I were speaking in a foreign language. After an uncomfortable pause, he could only respond with, "But then Burger King would have a cheaper burger. We'd lose market share."

Sigh.

I wasn't surprised he reacted this way. It's the kind of attitude that's all too common among both for-profit and nonprofit leadership. People are too afraid to take new opportunities to think differently, for fear of losing ground. But it's that very inaction and inability to think creatively that infects these older organizations. When Ray Kroc started McDonald's, he didn't have to worry about market share, because he created the market. Ford didn't care what the Dodge brothers believed, because he believed in himself.

Times have changed, and now there's a chance for McDonald's to radically shift the way the majority of the world sees it, or for Ford to be in the forefront of environmentally responsible automobiles. But both companies, like most larger and older nonprofits, have too much at stake, too much invested, too much infrastructure, to take the kind of big public chance that would demonstrate a core commitment to a cause.

At this point, every move is calculated based on whether it'll generate more profit. Every decision comes from the head, not from the heart.

When are nonprofit organizations and companies like Ford and McDonald's going to realize that we're smarter than they give us credit for? We can tell when someone's being genuine and when he's pretending. Just watch any presidential debate. We've seen every pitch, spin, and angle to convince us of something. We know when a company is trying to appear socially responsible just to sell more products, and when a nonprofit is trying to sell pity, not a plan.

So it begs the question: Where's the next Iggy Pop?

Iggy had the kind of in-your-face, take-it-to-11 attitude that we should all have in the nonprofit sector. Back in the early '80s, when Iggy came to D.C. to perform, I bought my tickets early. He was one of the few performers I'd go out of my way to see, and he didn't let us down. Shirtless, tight, raw and full bore, Iggy flew the stage of the Bayou in Georgetown like a black hawk swooping over its prey.

At one point during the show, someone from the balcony let out the biggest gob of spit toward the stage. You could follow the trajectory of this projectile as it flew on its way toward Iggy. Closer and closer it came, until everyone realized that it was going to land right on Iggy's fine kisser. And so it did, in all its glory.

Never in all of history has a loogie been more accurately aimed. It hit Iggy dead center, on the right side of his face, and it proceeded to run fast down his cheek.

No flinch, no wipe. Nothing but taking it like a great performer and kicking out the jams harder than ever with the Sales

Brothers pounding out the rhythm of "I'm Bored." I was anything but. It was the finest piece of punk ethos I've ever seen.

This wasn't a "the show must go on" attitude. This kind of thing WAS the fucking show. Call it integrity or intestinal fortitude or audacity, Iggy had the right stuff to go with the flow and push his performance as far as possible.

We can't all take it as hard as Iggy, but we can learn a thing or two from his performance style. Whether we're part of a company or a nonprofit, we have to be dedicated enough to our cause to be able to take the hits. Risk equals reward. Taking a chance means that there's stuff flying at you, and when that happens you need to be able to take it on the face and still perform with the utmost audacity. Ford was sued by the Dodge brothers, Ray Kroc took a second mortgage on his house to start McDonald's at the age of 54, and Bernie Glassman converted a small bakery into a multimillion-dollar operation. These individuals had the audacity to take things to the next level.

It's our job—every generation's job—to spit, and in turn be spit upon. It's our duty to question everything our older generations have done, and in turn to allow younger generations to question what we've done. David Bowie reminded us in his song "Changes" that the children we spit upon are immune to our consultations. They're here to challenge us and to question the status quo. Both Bowie and Iggy showed us in their lyrics and their performances what it meant to take on the establishment, and what it took to take it to 11 every time they stepped on stage. They knew that in order to make hits, you had to know how to take hits.

CHAPTER 10

Keeping the Faith

Brace yourself for elimination/or else your hearts must have the courage for the changing of the guards.

—BOB DYLAN, "Changing of the Guards"

No kid ever says, "When I grow up, I want to be a boring, overpaid executive of an ineffective nonprofit." Yet it happens all the time. Why? Because people get complacent. They fall into routines and lose sight of what drives them. Routine is the enemy. Whether it's love, business, friendship, once routine sets in, you're in big trouble. And one of the great lessons in my life that hammered this home was the week I spent with Sarah Vaughan while I was managing Charlie's in Georgetown.

Sarah and Ella were two of the greatest voices of the 20th century. They were like the yin and yang of jazz. Ella was a happy, scatty, vibrant performer, while Sarah was a quiet, emotive, operatic star.

By the early '80s, Ella had retired from the music scene, her legs all but shot from diabetes. Sarah was still on the road, still packing in crowds wherever she went, still singing her signature songs. Around the twilight of her career, I was just beginning my experience as a club manager, and although I had already seen a legend or two come to Charlie's, Sarah was more than that. She and Billie Holiday were jazz goddesses of the first order. In the history of jazz, she was one of the apostles. She had been there at every major moment.

And her price tag befitted her stature: $35,000 a week. That was a lot of ducats for a club, even in the heyday of the '80s. In the parlance of the trade, we had to shake some booty to make this nut.

Charlie's was the kind of first-class joint that let you relax and see a show. There was going to be none of that "Sit down, shut up, two drinks, show's over, out you go" roll at Charlie's. But Sarah was the first truly marquee performer, and she was costing us a ton to bring in. At $35,000, we had to have two shows a night and push the service harder than we'd ever pushed.

On top of everything else, every investor who had ever put a dime into Charlie's was coming out of the woodwork with guests. They wanted the best damn seats in the place. The saying "The customer comes first" came in second when Sarah came to town. Investors came first, then regulars, then customers.

Imagine my position. People lined up outside the piano bar, waiting to see Zeus's daughter, thinking they were first in line at the escalator to Olympus. I had the dubious honor of opening the door and telling all those in line, "I'm sooooo sorry, sir, that seat is reserved."

It was one of the most stressful times at Charlie's, but all of my anxiety melted away when Sarah took the stage for the first time. It was something out of a movie, a smoke-filled stage and a dimly lit room. Sarah's band members were already in position, quietly adjusting their instruments, warming up their fingers and chops. Then everything went quiet. A spotlight came on and shone down on a single stool and a mike stand. Sarah walked out from the wing, dressed in a bronze sequined gown. She practically glided on stage and took a seat in the spotlight, looking like a work of art.

As soon as she opened her mouth, it sounded as if we were in the company of an angel. The woman could sing. I won't even try to describe her voice, except that what came out of her mouth was something close to liquid silky smoke. It curled out from the stage and wrapped around each audience member like a warm feather boa.

In my years at Charlie's, I felt fortunate seeing many jazz greats, getting to know them, even on occasion getting to pepper them with questions about the clubs they remembered, what made those joints better than the rest. I loved the classy Rosemary Clooney, laughed at the brassy Carmen McRae and stared in silence at Astrud Gilberto, the "Girl from Ipanema," whose show was so uninspired and lackluster we took to calling her the "Corpse from Ipanema." I laughed to Mort Saul and Steve Allen. I marveled at Bobby Short's amazing renditions of Cole Porter and watched in stunned silence as Oscar Peterson rode the 10-foot Bosendorfer like a trick pony.

But that night, Sarah's first night, was a new experience for me. I felt like the luckiest young man on the planet. I was in love. I understood the hype and why generations of listeners had made this woman a living legend.

Charlie's killed during the first show. Everyone in the audience was pumped because it was Sarah's first performance in Washington, D.C., in a long time. They ordered bottles of Dom and snifters of Rémy, they dined on prime rib and lobster. We were expecting another good turn for her late performance.

When Sarah took to the stage for the second time that night, a similar reverent hush fell over the new, late-night crowd, and a big smile spread across my face. I told myself, I can't believe I get paid to stand here and watch Sarah Vaughan!

But when she opened her mouth, something unexpected happened. Out came the same song, sung the same way. Then the same banter and the same jokes. She even performed the same "improvised" moment in the middle of the set, when the bass player started riffing in between songs and Sarah pretended to be hearing it for the first time. "Ooh, that's good," she said to the bassist. "Keep on with that." Their impromptu groove, it turns out, was staged for every performance. There wasn't a single spontaneous moment in the evening.

Sarah was phoning it in.

Sarah did the exact same show twice a night for six straight nights. Don't get me wrong, even phoning it in, Sarah

Vaughan was incredible. But by the end of the week, *I* could have done her set.

And amazingly enough . . . I found myself bored with her performance by the end of the week.

That's when I realized that if Sarah Vaughan could get boring, if her routine could become routine, what chance did the rest of us have? I realized that with love, with family, with friendship, with life, routine is the enemy. It's capable of fucking up all that's good. And no matter how much Sarah Vaughan was a legend, no matter how good her first performance was, my lasting memory of her was going to be colored by her routine.

You can't keep selling the same way over and over again. You constantly have to be changing, and you can't forget that you're also selling a product, whether it's yourself, your mission, or your business. There's how you do it, but there's also how you project it. You need to keep both fresh. Unless you're Sarah Vaughan, you *have* to keep it fresh, or you will perish.

When I took over as interim CEO of the United Way of D.C., I was replacing a man who'd left his position after only 19 months. Even though the United Way of D.C. was suffering from a poor public image and a bloated staff, the CEO had increased the staff by nearly 40 employees and raised the administrative costs of the organization from 9 percent to 15 percent.

His transgressions would have been bad enough had we not spent the last 10 years getting over the controversy of William Aramony, the United Way of America's stunningly complacent CEO who was forced to leave his position in 1992. Back then reporters had revealed the life of excess that Aramony led. He earned more than $450,000 in salary and benefits, had access to a condominium in New York City and a town house in Florida, and enjoyed traveling across the Atlantic on the expensive Concorde jet. When he first took the United Way position in 1970, he told friends and colleagues he'd probably stay for 10 years. Twenty-two years later, he was forced out by public outrage over his spending habits.

What happened? How could these two men, each of whom, one must assume, had entered the field full of promise, vision, and integrity, lose sight of their sense of purpose as stewards of public money? Like many others in the nonprofit world, they probably fell into a routine. They grew accustomed to earning healthy salaries without having to prove themselves year after year. While corporate executives have to report to shareholders, investors, and bankers, and public officers are accountable to their voters, nonprofit executives have no oversight except from their board of directors. As long as the executives manage their relationships with board members, there's little that can be done to hold an executive accountable.

Over many decades the United Way had established credibility among corporate and public donors. The generations of workers before us were proud to raise money at their offices for their annual United Way campaigns. They wanted to become campaign coordinators for their office fund-raising and watch the familiar fund-raising thermometer grow.

But business in America shifted, and corporations stopped giving the United Way their best and brightest. Campaign coordinators felt more obligation than devotion to the cause. Employees began to feel coerced or were made to feel guilty by their bosses if they didn't donate. Resentment toward this system grew. Fewer people wanted to help with the campaign, and fewer people wanted to give. Eventually, younger generations came into the workforce completely unfamiliar with the role the United Way played in their community. There was no value added to donating to the United Way rather than giving directly to a specific organization.

You have to think there's a tipping point in the career of a nonprofit executive when the person begins to believe in his or her own entitlement. He or she feels deserving of mammoth six-figure salaries and perks usually reserved for corporate CEOs. As author Thomas Sowell puts it, the preservation of a vision becomes "inextricably intertwined with the egos of those who believe in it." It's not that executives shouldn't earn money. It's okay to cash in. Just don't sell out.

How much money can you justify paying yourself if you're working at an organization whose mission is to help feed poor, hungry, and homeless people? How can you empathize with people you're trying to serve if you're making 10 to 20 times what they're making and your lifestyle is so foreign to theirs? How can you be a good leader of your organization if you can't empathize with your clients? In an ideal world, the directors of service organizations would have a salary commensurate with the organization's mission and client base.

In my case, as the executive director at the Kitchen, I felt comfortable making $55,000 a year. Guidestar, an online resource for nonprofits and donors, reports that the average salary of a male CEO of a nonprofit is $70,820. But CEOs of organizations with operating budgets above $5 million annually make well over $100,000 a year.

If politicians have salary and term limits as public servants, shouldn't the directors and board members of nonprofits (including foundations) establish similar guidelines too? Executives should be judged at regular intervals by a set of criteria agreed upon by the board. Every administrator should have to demonstrate on a regular basis why he should keep his job. And he should take his case to the people who fund the nonprofit's programs, as well as to the people these programs serve.

Nonprofit managers, similarly, should have a system of checks and balances for their boards to ensure proper oversight of an organization. If a board member sits on more than three boards, can he focus on his duties at any one organization? Or if a board member has been in his position for more than 10 years, can he still look at the organization with fresh eyes and a clear perspective? Without creative conflict to shape the strategy of an organization, you end up with a panel of yes-people too afraid or too comfortable to think and act in the best interest of the organization. Ultimately, the organization becomes static, loses effectiveness, and fails to evolve with its changing environment.

The same rules apply to work, home, family, and friends. Whenever I speak at colleges, I like to remind students that you have to work at your friendships. I tell them that these are the best friends many of them will have in their lives, but just because they're best friends in college doesn't mean they'll be best friends forever. Flames always flicker out unless you give them fuel. I tell them that life is tough, and that it will rob many of them of their passion and wild beliefs. They'll need each other as they grow, to remind themselves of what they believed in to remember why they fight, love, and need to keep the home fires burning. That's one of the reasons I send postcards to old friends and colleagues. I break the routine in my day to break the routine in their day.

They say love is not a feeling. It's a dedication, a way of life. If you love what you do, you have to find ways to avoid the routine that makes us complacent.

Let me give you one more example. There's a young woman I know named Jill. She is the epitome of her generation. I met her when she came to work for a year at the Kitchen as an AmeriCorps volunteer. Like most peers in her age group, she has volunteered in her community since she was in high school. Like many of her age, she carried that spirit through college and into her early 20s, when she embarked on a journey to learn, grow, and serve. That led her to our door, where she helped to build our street outreach program, First Helping, and to supervise our first Summer Food program. She was also chosen to help President and Mrs. Clinton prepare lasagna for about 2,000 when they visited the Kitchen in 1998.

After her time in AmeriCorps, Jill joined the Peace Corps and served in Madagascar. She returned to the States with a new sense of purpose and vision, armed with a soul that had been tempered by the sights, sounds, and smells of poverty and death, but equally infused with the joy and earthly beauty that one finds so often intertwined in close-knit rural communities.

Now she is, like thousands of her contemporaries, ready for the next step. Like many of her time who've given in a thousand different ways, in a thousand different communities, she now wants to contribute to the larger dialogue. She wants to dig in and work at an agency or for a program that will let her brimming brain be part of making big change happen.

You could make a case that Jill is like thousands of young

Americans, in all sectors of our economic scale, who are trying to find their place in the world. But I've met thousands of Jills in my nonprofit journeys who've invested years in learning and serving.

And they are hitting a real wall.

They're looking for an organization that takes full advantage of what they have to offer, not of them. They want a job that not only challenges them but rewards them—not just in monetary ways but in meaningful, heartfelt ways. And in search of this elusive goal, they bounce from job to job, hunting down that mix of passion, mission, and lofty goals.

What they want is basic when you get down to it. They want less talk and more action. They want their leaders to work side by side with them, not direct them from third-floor office suites. They want leaders who are focused more on the people we serve, not the funders they court. They want integrity and openness, and more than anything else, they want to be inspired. They want to believe that they can preserve the passion of their young hearts while getting smarter and braver about how they turn that energy into action. They want to follow, but not to just earn a check or to be counted as a vote. No, they want to be part of an army that uses the resources of this world for the good of the many, not the desires of a few. They aren't communists or socialists, capitalists or radicals. . . . They are simply a generation of kids we've raised to do community service. Like the mothers who are leaving welfare and getting their first jobs, they are doing just what we asked them to do. They are the new American fighters, a ragtag army of true believers that we've been arming for the last decade, and they itch for a fight. They are poised for greatness, if some of us would just get out of the way and some of us just show them the way.

And there are more of them coming. Thousands more every year are graduating from high schools and colleges, armed with love and loaded for bear.

What are we waiting for?

Like coaches, we must help train the young sprinters to become long-distance runners. Too many are burning out, too fast. Too many are getting complacent. Some of them leave the sector; others try to start their own nonprofits without the proper training to make it over the long haul. We can't afford to have invested so much in our young leaders only to have them burn too brightly, too early.

We have to let them know that the long road of direct service work isn't easy. In fact, we have to let them know that it's going to be damn hard. We need to help them see the need to have balance in life if they're going to be able to handle the heat. Family, exercise, dancing, poetry, tequila . . . there are a thousand ways to let it out. Help them find the way that works for them, so they can work for you and for us.

Teach them that passion can best be preserved when tempered with patience and strengthened through persistence. Talk is cheap. Show them that, through your actions and your commitment. Be an example. Admit it when you are wrong, and give them credit when they are right.

Most of all, train them to train those that will follow. Someone once said that a good leader doesn't create more followers. Good leaders create more leaders. I say amen to that.

Does your town have a leadership program? If not, start one today. If your town does, make sure there is a program for young leaders. And then be a part of it, NOW. Invite these young leaders to your board meetings or strategic planning sessions. Take as many under your wing as possible. Be a guide. Introduce them to your partners. Let them see that you still believe, and help them learn how to keep the fire alive. Let them see how you make decisions, and how good deals and realistic compromises are made. Help them learn why the world is sometimes gray, versus black and white. But teach them to see the future in Technicolor.

We can't all be Sarah Vaughan. We have to try harder to break the daily monotony. We have to rid the sector of complacency and reward the individuals—young and old—who want to stir things up and break the routines. Sarah Vaughan once sang a beautiful version of "Send in the Clowns." It's too late for nonprofits. They're already here. Let's send them on their way and keep the sector fresh.

CHAPTER 11

Grab the Future by the Face

An excellent plumber is infinitely more admirable than an incompetent philosopher. The society that scorns excellence in plumbing because plumbing is a humble activity and tolerates shoddiness in philosophy because it is an exalted activity will have neither good plumbing nor good philosophy. Neither its pipes nor its theories will hold water.

—JOHN GARDNER, *Excellence*

When you're doing biz in the nonprofit sector you have to have split vision—what you do today has to be able to be done with an eye toward changing the future. Look at what's coming down the road, but also don't lose sight of what's in front of you.

It's not enough to see the future coming—you have to go out today and meet it, confront it, challenge it, change it. And there is no time like the present to begin.

Back in 1989, food was plentiful. Americans wasted or threw away an astonishing 25 percent of ALL the food produced in this country, every day. We're talking billions of pounds of food, more than enough to feed everyone who's hungry in America and then some. Getting food for the hunger cause was like fishing in a stocked pond. Food banks were filled with the overflow from the American food system. Companies like Kraft, General Mills, and Kellogg's donated tons of surplus nonperishable products that for one reason or another didn't pass their inspectors. Restaurants, hotels, and convention centers donated tons of perishable food, with no end in sight. Gleaning groups regularly brought in truckloads of fresh fruits and vegetables culled from fields around our cities.

We used to joke at the Kitchen when George Bush Sr. was in power that caterers had a saying: "Roast beef and shrimp and keep it coming!"

For a few years it all seemed so easy. It was only a matter of distributing everything we received. But while the newly minted social crusader in me realized that hunger wasn't about food, the old restaurateur in me couldn't stop thinking about supply, demand, and the inevitability of change.

Now I look out on the nonprofit sector and see that yesterday's emergencies (homelessness, hunger, drug addiction, AIDS) have become today's routine. Like hapless UN troops, we are monitoring a bad peace, waiting to react to the flare-ups that are inevitable. Too many of us in the direct-service end of the biz have long since quit fighting as if "we're trying to put ourselves out of business," as the old nonprofit mantra goes. Rather, we are fighting—and often with each other—just to keep our businesses afloat. And while we're preoccupied, everything about our world is changing.

This has got to stop, because when we are diverted, by routine or internecine warfare, we not only miss opportunities that are here today, but are blinded to the changes and challenges that are sure to come tomorrow.

We need to be constantly thinking, anticipating, and planning. Whom do we serve now; whom will we serve in the future? What will we serve them? Where will we serve them? Who will help us? How much will it cost? Can we prevent or decrease demand? Does the public share our concern, and see what we see? Do we see what it sees and share its concerns?

Like any industry, we cannot assume anything will last. We cannot become complacent or comfortable with the status quo, or get into maintenance mode. There is too much at stake, and not just socially and economically. If we are going to really change things, we'll have to really think this through, like any business. And like any business, it invariably comes down to the law of supply and demand.

Let's begin with supply and go from there.

I love asking volunteers or visitors to the Kitchen what the bountiful food that they see surrounding them means to the businesses that donated it. "A tax deduction" is a usual first response. Some suggest that it saves money on trash removal, improves employee morale, or makes them look good to their customers. These are all legitimate answers. But it's more basic than that.

Donated food is lost profit.

And because of that, it is inevitable that restaurants, caterers, and manufacturers will find better ways to preserve their food, and more efficient ways to order and deliver this food. And for an industry that runs on donations, and that has constituents that depend on it for food, supply is about a lot more than the proverbial bread and butter.

So as the food-service industry gets tougher on its bottom line, the Kitchen, and the antihunger movement in general, will have to develop systems that will maximize the food we have today.

Breedlove, a nonprofit based in Lubbock, Texas, has been working to address that problem. Around 10 years ago the founders raised millions of dollars to build a giant food-dehydration plant that would preserve vegetables in easily shippable, easily storable bags. One of the biggest problems at any community kitchen is spoilage, so by dehydrating vegetables like carrots, onions, and celery, and adding nutritional supplements, Breedlove not only had come up with an answer to the waste problem; it also had a solution for fighting malnutrition. Dehydrated food, sealed for a long shelf life with added nutrients, was going to be one of the most valuable weapons in our war against hunger.

Today Breedlove has distributed more than 50 million servings of dehydrated food to Third World countries all over the globe. It's hasn't quite caught on in this country (Americans aren't crazy about eating dehydrated food), but Breedlove's been able to stay with its cause of fighting hunger by moving overseas with its product.

Across the state from Breedlove, the North Texas Food Bank in Dallas tried a different alternative in its community kitchen. They began to experiment with flash freezing. That way, the tractor trailer of tomatoes that would have had to be distributed immediately can now be made into tomato sauce and then frozen in one- and five-gallon containers. When cooks combine it with pasta, eggplant, and cheese, they can make lasagna, and freeze that. Corn becomes corn chowder or part of a succotash.

Similarly, we've looked at other ways to increase supply.

In the mid-1990s, the Department of Agriculture, led by Dan Glickman, created valuable programs that helped corporations donate more easily to nonprofits. The Food Donor and Donee Act of 1998, signed by President Clinton in a Rose Garden ceremony, made it possible for national companies like Marriott, Sodexho, Pizza Hut, and KFC to develop national donation policies, which gave us the ability to move beyond local restaurants and caterers and gain access to big-time producers of surplus food like universities and corporate dining facilities.

It may make some wince, but many East Coast programs now work with local fish and game officials to access protein following organized deer hunts. Again, many balk at the prospect of killing Bambi, but venison is a solid source of protein that we can't ignore.

Nor can we ignore the nutritional value of the food we serve today, lest we create more problems for ourselves. It's ironic that a hunger crusader is concerned with people getting too fat, but the issues of hunger and obesity are tied together. In a country that produces 3,800 kilocalories of food per person, per day (nearly twice as much as needed for an adult), more than 127 million Americans are overweight, 60 million are obese, and 9 million are severely obese. The World Health Organization has named obesity one of its top 10 global health problems.

Am I worried about fat homeless people? No. But I am worried about productivity in this country. I am worried about our tax base. And I do worry about the impact of an impaired and unhealthy workforce, as well as the impact of other sensitive areas such as the 600,000 foster children who are aging out of the system, and the 2 million criminals who are packed in our overcrowded prison systems, many of whom will return to their hometowns looking for an opportunity to make a living.

But do you want to know my biggest worry? Two words: baby boomers. We represent that illustrious group of Americans born between 1945 and 1963 . . . the big daddy of all age groups—and that leads us to the next topic, demand.

There are about 74 million boomers that are going to be aging out of the workforce over the next 30 years. And here's the most impressive factoid you'll read in this book: The first boomer will officially turn 60 a few seconds past the stroke of midnight, January 1, 2005. Now we know that many of them will work well into their 70s and even 80s at the end of what will undoubtedly be a longer life span. Millions of them will depend on service agencies for meals and medicine and other essential needs. How can we hope to address this demand when the most prominent food-delivery agency for the elderly, Meals on Wheels, has a waiting list for 40 percent of its locations? That means almost 1,300 Meals on Wheels programs in this country are not able to meet the demands of their community—today. What's going to happen when the donor pool shrinks and the boomers expand the need? Who will be ready to take on that demand if we can't meet the goals today?

The plot thickens: Not only will there be less food to use and more people (who are less mobile) to serve, but the tax base will have a modest percentage of its workers impaired by issues related to diet, which will put further strain on the health system. If so many adults are obese today, and the numbers continue to rise, imagine what kind of problem we're going to have in 25 years. Again, it's split vision. We have to see what's taking place now and anticipate what's going to get better or worse in the future.

To start, we need to ask ourselves, our employees, our colleagues, our partners, our friends, and even our spouses some simple questions: Why do we keep doing the things we do if there's no real change or improvement? Is there a better way, and if there is, how do we get there?

If you're one of the millions of leaders out there fighting for social reform, start this revolution by telling us the how and why of what you're doing, not just the who and what. We need to hear from you. For the past 20 years Paul Newman has donated more than $125 million to charity from his Newman's Own company. He sells great food for great causes and he's raised a hell of a lot of money. But can you name a single charity he donates to, or the ways in which his money has been used to help address social problems at their core? Imagine if he told you the *how* and *why* of his giving history. That's the difference between 19th-century charity and 21st-century community building. Think about Ben & Jerry's. The company is one of the best-known socially responsible businesses in this country. But

BEGGING FOR CHANGE

161

do you know where their money is going? Neither do we, but in learning more about their social agenda, we can become smarter and more effective in helping the causes they support. This new level of engagement is where the realms of advocacy and action overlap. Every action a nonprofit takes should be a form of advocacy, and every type of advocacy should be linked with a type of action.

From now on, giving isn't enough. Philanthropy has to take itself to the next level by demanding results from what's given and taken. We've already been down the road of using money as a metric. Charity for the 21st century is about the ways in which we use money—and other resources—to get the maximum long-term results in whatever or whomever we're trying to help. If the 20th century was all about bucks, the 21st century has to be about what kind of bang we can get from these bucks.

Remember Pioneer Human Services? It generates $50 million a year in revenues and has one of the best business models of any human service nonprofit in the country. Yet most of America has never heard of it. Organizations like Pioneer need to get in front and market themselves like never before. They need to shout out from the mountaintop so that everyone down below can see and hear them. They need to be that beacon, that lighthouse in the storm, so that others find their way.

As we continue forward, we need education, motivation, and inspiration from every faction and every part of our society. Individuals, nonprofits, and corporations all have to get more vocal and more transparent about the good deeds they do. The public needs to be able to see if a company is posturing with cause-based marketing merely to look good—and sell more products—or because it really cares about fighting for the cause. We need more than just talk. We need to see the cause and effect of the company's actions.

On the nonprofit side, we have to ask ourselves tough questions. We have to challenge one another to look for ways to improve our missions, to consolidate—not duplicate—services, and to share brain wealth in the cheapest ways possible. Look at any major city and you'll find a similar pattern: larger inner-city nonprofits have been around for at least 20 to 30 years, while smaller, younger nonprofits in the suburbs and outer rings have been around maybe five to 10 years. Is it any surprise that these younger organizations seem to be more effective in fighting for their causes? Ask yourself if the older organizations in your city have adapted their missions to fit with the changing times or whether you see the managements at these organizations constantly pushing themselves and their nonprofits to stay fresh after all of these years. How many of them can achieve efficiency and oversight with 30 to 40 members on their board? How many have staff lists and office buildings that rival those of any large local business? Which of these older organizations have grown complacent, or are more vested in keeping the status quo rather than winning their war?

How many services in your community would benefit if nonprofits consolidated their services with other agencies, or enlisted volunteer middle management to help provide expensive professional services. How would nonprofits benefit from free accounting work, IT support, or management training? How many aging workers would love to donate their work skills as a way of giving, rather than performing the typical volunteer tasks of serving meals or mentoring children?

How many national associations that were created decades ago at a time of real need no longer have that same reason for being in an age of cyber-organizations? Our coalition, Kitchens, INC (Kitchens in National Cooperation), is a free association of more than 75 community kitchens around the country. There are no dues, no large overhead, and only one full-time staff member on the payroll to maintain the association. Members share advices, ideas, and emotional support directly with each other without dealing with the red tape, dues, or infrastructure of a third-party association.

On the business end, we need to recognize that corporations are going to be the drivers of real change in philanthropy in the future. Altria, for example, currently funds Meals on Wheels, AIDS kitchens, and community kitchens all around the country. Will Altria continue funding all three groups, each with its own accountant, executive director, and annual budget, in perpetuity? Of course not. Altria is going to demand reform in these areas to get better return on its spending. It has to and will become a much more vocal and active participant that demands the consolidation of these services. The alternative is for Altria to face another 50 years of being flooded by an overwhelming deluge of grant proposals from organizations, most of which need to be merged or eliminated.

Back at the turn of the 20th century, Carnegie and Rockefeller paved the way for generations of successful business leaders to create a pattern of philanthropy: Make much money in business, and then later in life try to redistribute this profit by giving it back to society.

But after seeing this formula carried out with little success for the past 100 years, we now know this: Carnegie and Rockefeller were looking at the wrong end of the equation. Ill-gotten gains produce an ill society. Rather than make hundreds of millions of dollars in profit by exploiting employees, competitors, and the market as Rockefeller did with Standard Oil, and rather than donating hundreds of millions of dollars back to society after you've attained this enormous wealth, the formula needs to be flipped around. To get to the root of society's problems, Rockefeller had to change the way he ran his business. Ford tried to do this by increasing the wages of his workers, but his other management tactics fell far short of corporate responsibility. And since their time, every business executive has followed this same formula.

I'd like to urge any CEO or director of a company who wants to help a person in need to start with your own people— your employees. Make sure they're taken care of and then work your way out in concentric circles, your neighborhood, your community, your city and state. Don't donate your time to the inner city if your own employees aren't making a living wage. Spend more time figuring out how to pay them better and provide more benefits, rather than constructing a golden parachute for your fellow executives. As the saying goes, if we all do with a little less, we all get a little more.

We have examples of corporate social responsibility all around us. We just need them to speak out more. Look at the outdoor company Timberland, which allows its employees to have 40 hours of paid leave to volunteer in their community. Or Target, which donates more than $2 million a week on education, arts, and social services. There's also SAS, the world's largest private software company, which treats its employees like family. At its headquarters in Cary, North Carolina, SAS provides employees with on-site health care, day care, fitness, and relaxation facilities. Everywhere you turn, companies are implementing more socially conscious policies because they realize that informing the public is no longer just good PR, it's good business. Once these companies show their competitors that purpose is an equal part of the equation, the entire corporate world will follow—with the government not too far behind.

We're at an exciting moment in the history of nonprofits and business, the confluence of for-profit and nonprofit ideologies. People no longer want companies to squeeze profit out of everything they do. They want purpose and meaning. They recognize the social responsibility everyone—even corporations—has in today's global environment.

As a result, profit *and* purpose have become a unified formula for running any organization. The formula is simple:

PURPOSE = PROFIT

No matter what type of organization you lead, whether it's nonprofit, for-profit, or governmental, the results should be the same. The more purpose you create, the more profit you'll generate; the more profit you generate, the more purpose you create. Companies and organizations that strive for social change can show us the possibilities of running a businesslike nonprofit, and a nonprofitlike business. And the marriage of these two ideas is our future.

This is not an invitation for businesses to take over the nonprofit sector. This is about people tapping into the same power Gandhi and King tapped into. It's about mobilizing the public into the most powerful agent of social change. It's how you, the American public, buy your products, how you spend your time and money. **Purpose = Profit.** It's about the power of people to use their money on every side of the transaction.

The final variable in this equation comes from neither the nonprofit nor the profit side, but from the government. Even though we have to reform the nonprofit sector and educate and inspire consumers and businesses, no matter how much we do on the outside, we'll never achieve permanent change in our society unless we get cooperation from the government.

Think about Habitat for Humanity and Rising Tide, two great groups we talked about earlier. They are two of the greatest sources of inspirational volunteerism that there are, but all they can really do, like the Kitchen, is highlight the larger challenge we have as a society. They, and all the housing groups out there put together, will never generate the kind of capacity required to meet the need, in any town, let alone any state or this country. This is a place for government. *Only* government can generate the kind of funding and legislation required to house our workers, our families, and all our would-be neighbors. Only government can generate the kind of change needed in our educational, child care, health care, and retirement systems.

I'm not advocating an expansion of government, but I am trying to get people to understand that government has to weigh in and define its role. Only when the government indicates how it will spend its money can we use our money more effectively. And while it should be our job to guide the government's allocation of taxes (start with your local chamber of commerce), we'll never be able to eradicate society's worst problems without the government.

So what comes at the end of this book is my plan. Okay, it's not so much a plan as it is a summary of everything I've touched on in this book and advice that I've gathered over the years. It's directed to each and every person out there. Think of it as "Robert's Rules of Engagement," or "Life's Little Non-profit Handbook."

Come up with some of your own and let me know. I want to hear from you. There's plenty of room here, and the view is great.

Redemption City

You may say I'm a dreamer, but I'm not the only one.
—JOHN LENNON, "Imagine"

There's a faint echo you can hear, if you put your ear to the ground in America.

It's the call of our youth.

It's the faint reverberation of the footfalls of thousands of men and women who had to put aside their youth to march off to war. It's the still-audible challenge of a president who asked the next generation to do more than ask for themselves. It's the echo of a singer who invited us to imagine, and the call of a minister who dared us to dream. And it's the mournful promises we made at the foot of their graves.

It's the crash of the waves on the shores of that endless summer that ended a long, long time ago, followed by the faint but steady beat of that different drummer we were going to march to.

And while the din of this world can make those words and sounds and memories seem to be merely the faint echo of what might have been, that's only because you listen for the sounds of your youth, the sounds that only you and your peers, your generational brothers and sisters, can recognize.

But what you don't discern is that if you could put all those echoes together, they would create a din that would deafen you.

And with all the impatience and longing and energy of those lost, lean, and lingering years, they would scream out two words: Build it!

Build that world we fought for, died for, marched for, worked for, howled for, paid taxes for, voted for, prayed for, and sang about. Build those communities, those schools, those businesses, that dream, that country.

Well, friends, I'm like that kid in *The Sixth Sense*. I hear those voices. And I know what I'm going to do with my life. If you want to join me, we can work together and build that shining city on the hill, Redemption City. We can do it, but only if we learn to work together.

When I took the job at the United Way in 2002, I had a vision of how this organization could use green to beat social problems black and blue. The United Way of the National Capital Area, in its best year, raised over $90 million from employees of area businesses. It operates in a community in which businesses alone will donate an additional $800 million to non-profits. Yet the two *never* talked. If you add in the resources of the local governments, and then, on top of that, federal subsidies . . . baby, we are talking billions of dollars annually. And still, nobody talks.

That was at the heart of my battle plan for the beleaguered agency. Not only could the United Way redefine its role, but through the process, it could redefine how we allocated all the money in Washington.

Now ours was a *unique* United Way. Over 90 percent of its income was designated, which meant that it was little more than a pass-through organization. Sure, it handled $90 million, but it did little with it. On a national level, the United Way system was beginning to focus on an "impact agenda." We decided that this was the direction for us, too.

But the power wasn't in trying to get folks to give us a bigger pie. It was in getting the community to realize that our take was merely the icing on a big-assed cake that could, proverbially, feed the entire community.

That is how I spent my entire tenure at the helm of the beaten and bruised United Way. Rather than defend what it was, I wanted to tell them what we could rebuild, together. I started to talk about the folks at the Atlanta United Way, and how they had organized citywide efforts to pool funds, put their heads together, define their goals, and get it *on*.

We started to pose questions to the groups we met. We started to talk about building a metaphorical ladder in our community. We asked what would be on the first rung if at the top was independence. Food, shelter, clothing, and child care usually came first. Education, health care, and transportation came next, followed by safety issues, workforce development, and civic issues like leadership development. We asked local chambers of commerce and church social groups. We asked nurses and cashiers, linemen and CEOs alike what they thought.

And while the organization has miles to go to regain its footing in Washington and regain the trust of this community, the process of engaging the donors in the process was *the* beginning. Not because they had any particular insight, but because it helped everyone see that we had to take it a step at a time, hand in hand. We couldn't teach a kid to read who hadn't eaten breakfast. You can't get someone a job if he or she is still using crack. First things first, and to each season a turn.

That's one of the roots of Redemption City. . . . It takes a village to raise a village, and it takes brains and hearts working simultaneously. We have to build strong rungs on the ladder. They must be clearly marked, and in the right order. They must be strong enough to hold those who must rest or who can climb no further, yet close enough to be within the reach of each of those on the way up.

I was reminded of the importance of this type of camaraderie when I went to address the graduates of a local program here in D.C. named Hoop Dreams. Developed by one of D.C.'s most enterprising young leaders, Susie Kay, the program provides scholarships to young men and women who are graduating from some of D.C.'s toughest high schools.

As I talked to the kids, I told them about one of my favorite historical figures, Harriet Tubman, whose grave I try to visit every year when I travel to upstate New York to speak at

Cornell and Syracuse. I wanted these kids to understand the difference between talking about a problem and actually putting yourself into the middle of the solution, and Harriet ranks at the top of my list in the pantheon of freedom fighters and activists.

During the abolitionist and women's suffrage movements of the mid-1800s, amazing speakers like Frederick Douglass, Sojourner Truth, and Susan B. Anthony traveled the highways and byways of the northern states, giving speeches and raising awareness of the endemic problems of slavery and subjugation. These men and women played a pivotal role in the fight, and their voices were crucial, but it took a Harriet Tubman to bring the fight home. She was willing to go deep into the South, where she had a $40,000 bounty on her head. If she were caught, she'd have been hanged from the closest tree. And at just a little over 5 feet tall, and weighing just over 100 pounds, it wouldn't have taken much of a tree to hang her from. Yet she went . . . again and again, 19 times, defying all odds, and risking life and limb with every step. When she was done, she had helped free more than 300 people, including all her family members.

To her charges, her rules were rigid and her pace grueling. She kept them moving from dusk to dawn, never letting any of them turn back and never losing a single person.

Harriet Tubman had the nerve, the bravery, and the devotion to get the job done. But what I love most about the story of Harriet Tubman is the password she used with members of the Underground Railroad. Whenever she came upon a house or a shelter and the person on the other side of the door asked who it was, she replied, "A friend with friends."

A friend with friends.

That's what it comes down to. People who not only walk the talk, but see the connection between their lives and the lives of everyone around them. We need more Harriets in this fight. And we need to understand what it means to be a friend with friends. We have to be in this effort together. We'll fight together, win or lose battles together, and celebrate together.

As a kid growing up, a child of my times and a full-blown hippie wanna-be, I knew the words to most of the songs I had ever heard. In some weird twist of fate, this talent puzzled my parents and confused every math teacher I ever had. I could remember the lyrics to every song that played on the radio but failed to the grasp the Pythagorean theorem, which, for heaven's sake, even the Scarecrow could blurt out five seconds after being handed a fake diploma by the Wizard of Oz.

But man, could I sing along with the rock stars. And the Beatles were *the* rock stars of my youth. Growing up in the U.S. in the '60s meant that every kid on every block bought the latest Beatles 45 or LP. As I came of age, and the simple "yeah, yeah, yeah's gave way to "coo, coo, ca joob," I remember the special joy my friends and I shared when Ringo would get the rare chance to sing. "I Get By with a Little Help from My Friends" was a song that everyone loved, and because Ringo was singing, *anyone* could sing. You didn't have to have a voice, just a heart.

As a young man, my understanding of friendship was pretty fraternal—a thing between the guys. I held on to this view into my 20s, until one night I was forced to rethink what I'd believed all my life.

Which brings us back to the Grate Patrol. As I looked

down at the long line of men waiting to be served, I thought about friendship, and how comfortable I had become in my universe. What a hypocrite I had been—singing about peace, love, and understanding, but not thinking about the meaning of the words. They were *my* peace, *my* love, *my* understanding—basically *my* world. I could sing, but could I act? I could strut, but could I stand? I could raise a fist, but would I lend a hand? Was I willing to offer my friendship to someone completely different, like one of the people I was serving?

That's when I began my search for the greater meaning of friendship. That's when I drew the line, and became aware that if I wanted to know the true meaning of friendship, I had to go out there and experience it firsthand.

For the past 15 years I've been a recovering hypocrite, and every day I've been working and sweating to make Washington, D.C., a better hometown, a place for friends with friends. You too can do your part in your city or town, even with your family, your neighborhood, your office or congregation. Don't be afraid to start small, or start with what you know best.

I hope his book has given you enough ideas and inspiration to set yourself on the right path if you feel you're not on it. For some of you, I hope you can begin to see at least that the path you've been on was put there by someone else. It may not lead ultimately to where you want to go.

If you're ever in the nation's capital, feel free to visit us at the D.C. Central Kitchen. Grab an apron, help the trainees cook some food, and then hang out with the many great people who work and train, laugh and play, and fight the battles of hunger and stereotypes. Until then, I'm sure I'll be caught up in a million new projects. Some of them will lead me toward a promised path; others will take me on a road to nowhere. No worries, though. I'll still be moving forward, and more than anything else, I'll be immersed in a project I've had my eyes set on for many, many years. I'm talking about something completely new and innovative and spectacular: the world's first nonprofit nightclub.

But I'll have to tell you more about that some other time. . . .

ROBERT'S RULES FOR NONPROFITS

- Look at what you do. Are you a 19th-century charity or a 21st-century community corporation?
- The recent downturn in public support for nonprofits isn't about the economy or 9/11. It's about skepticism. The public has had enough with pity and platitudes. Americans want a plan.
- As John Gardner says, it's better to be an excellent plumber than a bad philosopher. The era of talk is over. Say what you'll do, and do what you say.
- Nirvana was a great band, but it's a terrible nonprofit mission statement. Pie-in-the-sky visions need to be replaced with ground-level goals.
- No matter how good you think you are, you aren't. Everybody and everything can and will be boring. Always be

open to opportunity to push farther and go faster . . . and bring as many people along for the ride as possible.

• Credibility isn't tied to money. It doesn't matter how much money you make or how much money you raise. It's how that money makes something happen in your community.

• The wage genie is out of the bottle. Donors want to know how much nonprofit executives make. Can you justify your salary?

• If you've been in the same nonprofit executive or leadership position for longer than you can remember, you need to regularly evaluate your effectiveness. Look yourself in the mirror and ask: "Can I still get it on *every day,* or is it time for me to get out of the way?"

• Find balance. Give yourself and your employees time to decompress. A nonprofit career is hard work, and everyone needs some space and time off.

• Be committed to mentoring and training younger generations of employees and volunteers.

• Don't participate in mediocrity. Be an aggressive builder in your community. Make sure every partnership, every policy, and every plan has teeth.

• Stay dedicated to a larger message. Serve your cause first, then clients, community, and constituencies will follow.

• Every community is loaded with assets that no one sees or no one's put together. Don't waste anything—not money, not resources, not services, not people.

• What we see as a problem can oftentimes be part of the solution.

• Make sure volunteers and donors see how their contributions help. Show them tangible links with their efforts.

They'll be so excited that they'll tell two friends, and they'll tell two friends, and so on, and so on. . . . Word-of-mouth has more marketing power than any direct-mail campaign, national advertisement, or corporate sponsorship.

•   You can't tell people what to think. People have to discover an idea on their own. Set the stage so that, through your daily work, you put people in a place where they see the impossible made plausible.

•   What you think is out of reach is right in front of you. You may think an idea won't work, but that's what keeps the others in line. Is that where you want to be . . . or out front? Your choice.

•   Be aware of the language you use. Are you elevating the dialogue about what you do and whom you serve, or are you relying on outdated images or desperate calls for help to keep the checks coming in?

•   Harriet Tubman dragged her charges through swamps and dark woods on her way North. It wasn't easy, but the final objective was always freedom. If you're a direct-service nonprofit are you helping the people you serve attain their freedom?

•   We are a house divided. Hunger isn't about food, homelessness isn't about housing, and poverty isn't about money. The issues are interconnected, yet we in the nonprofit sector think and act otherwise. Until we create a dialogue to share ideas and devise a unified, sectorwide strategy, we'll continue to be ineffective, and our clients will stay disenfranchised.

•   Beware of the client caste system. When you put kids at the top that means someone's at the bottom. Don't create false priorities or give the public a choice they don't have to make.

The problems we seek to address are always wrong, no matter which group is affected.

• Administrative overhead is the wrong barometer to measure our efficiency. Don't be afraid to talk to your donors, your constituencies, and your community for the need to have strong administrative oversight and visionary planning.

• We're the only culture in the world that shows such little respect for our elders. Retiring boomers must be engaged, not disengaged from our society.

• Changing the world isn't a nine to five business. Volunteers and clients need programs that operate with *their* needs in mind.

• Hunter S. Thompson says, "When the going gets weird, the weird turn pro." Some of the best things happen when the train's moving too fast to jump off. Reward only comes with risk.

• My friend Brendan Canty of the band Fugazi says, "What's too loud?" If you're in the business of helping others, making things happen or building communities, super-size everything you do. Get bigger and louder.

• If you chase money, you'll be on an endless loop. If you chase results, the money will come.

Rules for Businesses

• Corporate philanthropy and nonprofit programs in this country are all over the map. Call a time-out, convene a gathering of all your local leaders, tally your resources, and coordinate the goals of your community. Then use your board of trade as a mechanism to lead change, to reevaluate where philanthropy is going, and to initiate a plan.

• Think of how much money we have in every community if we pooled money from the United Way, corporate philanthropy, individual donations, and the local government. Throw in the volunteer hours of students, corporate employees, and retirees. Add all of this up. Now tell me . . . with all of these resources, what can't we fix?

• Forget the three-year plan. Those are baby steps. Think Coltrane: *Giant Steps.* Imagine what your community will look like in 10 years. Combine your resources and your ideas, prioritize your plans, and work toward those goals as a true community.

• Don't try to reinvent philanthropy. Just as there are too many nonprofits duplicating services, there are too many corporations and foundations duplicating philanthropic efforts. Philanthropy has to be tied to local politics and partners in the community. If the players are not in sync, their efforts won't work.

• Don't get caught up in the glamour of giving. Even with the fastest computers or the latest educational software, you'll never successfully mentor a kid who hasn't first eaten a good meal. Take the ladder one rung at a time.

• Don't confuse marketing with making a difference. It's more important for the public to respect you than it is to like you. The public wants more than feel-good imagery. They want action.

• Carnegie and Rockefeller had it backward. Work from the inside out. Don't wait to be a millionaire before spreading the wealth to the less fortunate. Take care of the less fortunate around you, now. Find ways to do good inside your business, then look to giving outside this circle.

• Be a true leader, and realize in the future that profit will be tied to purpose.

• Consultants are fine, but for heaven's sakes, ask those who are already working for the cause what *they* need.

• By marketing the *how* and *why* of your philanthropy, you can help the public focus on giving. An educated public can be corporate philanthropy's strongest ally.

Rules for Volunteers and Donors

• Don't feel guilty if you can't fund every struggling or failing nonprofit. There are too many agencies chasing the same dollars, and the reality is we'd be stronger and more effective if many of them consolidated or went out of business.

• Americans give on average $1,600 a year to nonprofits. Would you invest that much in the stock market without doing research? Ask questions. Demand answers.

• Don't give to any organization that sets up the problem and not the solution. Remember, pity isn't a plan.

• Don't be fooled by fund-raising numbers and false percentages. Just because 100 percent of your donation goes to a cause, your money may not be actually helping the cause.

• Nonprofits are businesses and salaries are important, but don't be afraid to ask for salary information of the highest-paid employees of a nonprofit. Determine if you think the salary levels are appropriate.

• No contribution is too small. Stay organized and motivated. Look what Gandhi did with salt, MLK with dimes, Caesar Chavez with grapes, and Chris and his daughter with sandwiches. Give what you can, when you can.

• Recognize the connection between consumption and compassion. The two are no longer mutually exclusive. Support businesses or products that show the link between profit and purpose. The way you spend your money—the power of capitalism—can ultimately decrease the need for charity in the first place.

• Don't give up on pooled giving. A steady check from a federated giving program like the United Way is an amazing tool that allows nonprofits to be strategic and to budget accordingly.

• You don't say "I love you" just to hear it back. Don't get bent out of shape if you don't get a thank you right away or if you're name is misspelled on a letter. Realize how much nonprofits struggle every day to make ends meet.

• Don't scatter your donations. Philanthropy is spread across too many interests. Be selective and be generous, and fund the nonprofit you choose at a level that allows the organization to focus on the mission, not the money.

• Do you participate in work, church, and volunteerism by going to three separate locations? Can you find a way to connect these activities so that you do good work, observe your faith, and follow your convictions no matter where you are?

- You don't have to choose between supporting a salesman or a saint. The best nonprofit directors are a little of both. Don't be afraid to invest in the crazy, the untried, the difficult to believe. Those are the very programs that break through and create change.

- Everybody can give; everybody has a role. It's natural to want to see impressive, immediate results when you give, but small things can add up fast. Robert Kennedy said in a 1966 speech to South African students: "Each time a man stands up for an ideal or acts to improve the lot of others, or strikes out against injustice, he sends forth a tiny ripple of hope, and crossing each other from a million different centers of energy and daring, those ripples build a current that can sweep down the mightiest walls of oppression and resistance."

- Believe in the impossible. We have the power to make this an amazing society . . . if we work together. Be part of it. Make waves.

Giving and Volunteering Statistics and Resources

Volunteering in the United States, 2000

Percentage of adults who volunteered	44%
Total number of adult volunteers	83.9 million
Average weekly hours per volunteer	3.6 hours
Annual hours volunteered	15.5 billion
Number of full-time employees equal to these hours	9 million
Estimated hourly value of volunteer time	$15.40 per hour
Total dollar value of volunteer time	$239.2 billion
Percentage of adults asked to volunteer	50%
Percentage of adults who volunteered when asked	71%

Giving in the United States, 2000

Percentage of households contributing to charity	89%
Average annual household contribution	$1,620
Percentage of household income given	3.1%
Average contribution among volunteering households	$2,295
Percentage of households asked to give	57%
Percentage of contributing households that gave when asked	61%

Reprinted with permission from the Independent Sector.

2002 Contributions:
$240.92 Billion by Type of Recipient Organization

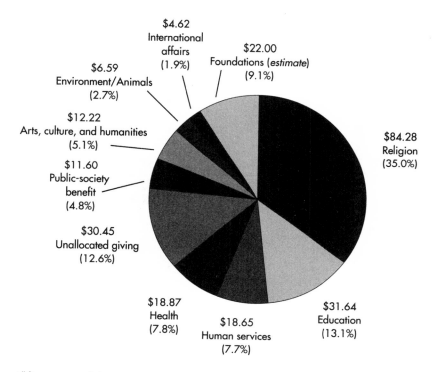

$4.62
International
affairs
(1.9%)

$22.00
Foundations (*estimate*)
(9.1%)

$6.59
Environment/Animals
(2.7%)

$12.22
Arts, culture, and humanities
(5.1%)

$11.60
Public-society
benefit
(4.8%)

$30.45
Unallocated giving
(12.6%)

$84.28
Religion
(35.0%)

$18.87
Health
(7.8%)

$18.65
Human services
(7.7%)

$31.64
Education
(13.1%)

All figures are rounded.
Total may not be 100%.

Source: AAFRC Trust for Philanthropy/*Giving USA 2003.*

2002 Contributions:
$240.92 Billion by Source of Contributions

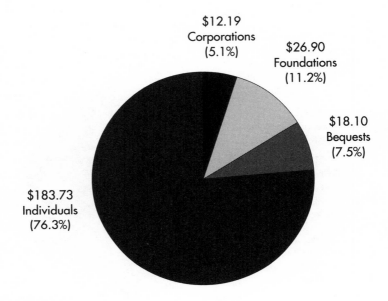

$12.19
Corporations
(5.1%)

$26.90
Foundations
(11.2%)

$18.10
Bequests
(7.5%)

$183.73
Individuals
(76.3%)

All figures are rounded.
Total may not be 100%.

Source: AAFRC Trust for Philanthropy/*Giving USA 2003.*

NONPROFIT COMPENSATION

Guidestar's 2002 compensation report draws on fiscal year 2000 Form 990 data from more than 65,000 public charities, and examines compensation by gender, 14 job categories, 9 budget categories, and 378 program categories. Information is also reported by state and for 254 metropolitan statistical areas.

Median CEO Compensation for Various Organization Types				
	Budget Size			
Organization Type	Greater Than $5,000,000	$1,000,000– $5,000,000	$500,000– $1,000,000	Less Than $500,000
Community Health Systems	$271,379	$120,523	$83,015	$57,751
University or Technological Institute	$189,990	$86,139	N/A	N/A
Art Museums	$188,621	$91,080	$62,000	$35,303
General Hospitals	$184,702	$80,126	N/A	N/A
Symphony Orchestras	$175,491	$70,035	$47,222	$28,841
Undergraduate Colleges (4-year)	$156,159	$77,004	N/A	N/A
Natural Resources, Conservation, Protection	$153,796	$82,707	$60,425	$40,217
Fund-raising Organizations	$137,543	$71,115	$46,000	$31,235
Animal Protection, Welfare	$128,116	$64,460	$44,618	$28,886
Community Mental Health Centers	$106,972	$75,764	$66,100	$49,063
Senior Continuing-Care Communities	$103,419	$66,150	$46,597	$33,946
Children's, Youth Services	$101,834	$69,528	$56,632	$37,500
YMCA/YWCA/YMHA/YWHA	$98,278	$73,954	$51,701	$36,156
Community, Neighborhood Development, Improvement	$89,540	$70,000	$60,953	$40,130
Human Services—Multipurpose	$87,796	$62,191	$48,967	$35,807
Child Day Care	$79,732	$60,210	$44,477	$28,801
Food Banks, Food Pantries	$66,375	$52,077	$46,789	$32,896

Source: *2002 Guidestar Nonprofit Compensation Report*

Median compensation was comparatively low in most human services organizations, ranking in the bottom 20 percent for each budget category. Housing and shelter organizations also ranked low.

There were sometimes large regional differences in CEO compensation. Salaries paid to CEOs of Mideast and New England nonprofits were highest for every budget size, with compensation in the Plains and Rocky Mountains regions typically the lowest. For example, the median compensation of CEOs at Mideast organizations with budgets of greater than $5 million was 25.7 percent higher than that of CEOs in the Plains region, and 18.1 percent higher than that of CEOs in the Rocky Mountains region.

CEO Compensation by Region and Budget Size				
	Budget Size			
Region	$500,000 or Less	$500,000–$1,000,000	$1,000,000–$5,000,000	Greater Than $5,000,000
Far West	$38,000	$56,523	$73,909	$125,000
Great Lakes	$36,712	$53,759	$72,059	$123,307
Mideast	$39,867	$60,000	$81,660	$138,817
New England	$39,524	$57,834	$78,293	$127,308
Plains	$35,842	$51,923	$69,409	$110,432
Rocky Mountains	$34,805	$51,695	$70,632	$117,595
Southeast	$36,044	$53,625	$71,492	$121,329
Southwest	$36,000	$51,864	$69,150	$120,789

Far West: AK, CA, HI, NV, OR, WA **Great Lakes:** IL, IN, MI, OH, WI **Mideast:** DE, MD, NJ, NY, PA, DC **New England:** CT, ME, MA, NH, RI, VT **Plains:** IA, KS, MN, MO, NE, ND, SD **Rocky Mountains:** CO, ID, MT, UT, WY **Southeast:** AL, AR, FL, GA, KY, LA, MS, NC, SC, TN, VA, WV **Southwest:** AZ, NM, OK, TX
Source: *2002 Guidestar Nonprofit Compensation Report*

Median CEO Compensation for Selected Metropolitan Areas

SMA	Budget Size $1,000,000–$5,000,000		Budget Size Greater Than $5,000,000	
	Raw Median	Adjusted for Cost of Living*	Raw Median	Adjusted for Cost of Living*
Baltimore, MD	$79,383	$79,862	$138,227	$139,061
Boston, MA	$86,715	$68,065	$152,182	$119,452
Cleveland, OH	$76,430	$74,493	$150,377	$146,566
Denver, CO	$80,000	$78,355	$137,592	$134,762
Detroit, MI	$74,375	$65,994	$124,959	$110,878
Los Angeles, CA	$80,901	$71,784	$148,414	$131,689
New York, NY	$91,748	$46,105	$159,663	$80,233
Phoenix, AZ	$75,430	$74,831	$117,441	$116,509
San Francisco, CA	$79,414	$52,453	$133,746	$88,339
Seattle, WA	$71,754	$63,725	$122,606	$108,886
St. Louis, MO	$75,756	$78,995	$144,353	$150,525
Washington, DC	$102,629	$85,311	$161,755	$134,460

* Cost of living data from Dowden & Co.
Source: *2002 Guidestar Nonprofit Compensation Report.*

	Female		Male		
Compensation by Gender and Job Category					
Job Category	Number	Median Salary	Number	Median Salary	Gender Gap
CEO/Executive Director	23,091	$50,554	29,063	$70,820	40.1%
Top Administrative Position	2,063	$62,099	2,080	$75,443	21.5%
Top Business Position	492	$61,125	673	$74,750	22.3%
Top Development Position	1,357	$68,053	1,568	$78,705	15.7%
Top Education/Training Position	246	$62,754	339	$72,923	16.2%
Top Facilities Position	33	$64,310	343	$69,321	7.8%
Top Financial Position	3,163	$61,716	5,557	$82,040	32.9%
Top Human Resources Position	480	$70,606	605	$90,728	28.5%
Top Legal Position	238	$79,092	489	$89,002	12.5%
Top Marketing Position	335	$70,109	452	$79,695	13.7%
Top Operations Position	904	$75,630	1,650	$94,873	25.4%
Top Program Position	1,137	$59,975	1,426	$65,951	10.0%
Top Public Relations Position	211	$69,387	288	$77,614	11.9%
Top Technology Position	178	$71,096	820	$85,837	20.7%

Source: *2002 Guidestar Nonprofit Compensation Report.*

To some degree, this disparity can be explained by the difference in the size of organizations at which men and women work. Of the 34,857 females in the report, 48 percent worked at organizations with budgets of $1 million or less, whereas only 32.1 percent of males worked at nonprofits of that size. On the high end, 22.9 percent of the females worked at organizations with budgets greater than $5 million, versus 38.5 percent of males. Even when controlling for the size of organization, however, women still earned less. As the table below shows, male CEOs at every budget level outearned their female counterparts in fiscal year 2000.

Compensation by Gender and Budget Size					
	Female		Male		
Budget Size	Number	Median Salary	Number	Median Salary	Gender Gap
$250,000 or less	5,977	$31,159	4,841	$36,274	16.4%
$250,000–$500,000	4,493	$41,487	3,787	$48,863	17.8%
$500,000–$1,000,000	4,182	$52,403	4,253	$60,000	14.5%
$1,000,000–$2,500,000	4,010	$64,953	5,455	$73,805	13.6%
$2,500,000–$5,000,000	1,976	$78,744	3,445	$89,500	13.7%
$5,000,000–$10,000,000	1,267	$91,179	2,793	$105,699	15.9%
$10,000,000–$25,000,000	759	$111,545	2,297	$135,937	21.9%
$25,000,000–$50,000,000	222	$143,188	890	$175,913	22.9%
More Than $50,000,000	205	$186,088	1,302	$271,032	45.6%

Source: *2002 Guidestar Nonprofit Compensation Report.*

Generally, male CEOs also earned more regardless of organization type. In the 114 program/budget categories with sufficient numbers of both gender to make meaningful comparisons, women earned more than men in only 11 categories. In K–12 education organizations with budgets of $250,000 to $500,000, the median compensation for women CEOs was 17.1 percent higher than that for men, the largest disparity in favor of women. The largest difference in favor of males was in hospitals with budgets greater than $50 million, where the median for males was 63.1 percent higher.

Reprinted with permission from Guidestar.

RESOURCES AND WEB SITES

D.C. Central Kitchen
425 Second Street NW
Washington, D.C. 20001
202-234-0707 phone
202-986-1051 fax
www.dccentralkitchen.org

Please visit the Web site or come to the kitchen in person to find the latest news and happenings at the Kitchen.

Kitchens, INC
1302 Walthour Road
Savannah, GA 31410
912-898-0595 phone
www.kitchensinc.org

Kitchens, INC is a coalition of more than 70 organizations dedicated to the free, open, and deliberate exchange of information for community-based training kitchens, their clients, and their partners. Kitchens, INC extends the mission of the D.C. Central Kitchen to "use food as a tool to strengthen bodies, empower minds, and build communities."

BBB Wise Giving Alliance
Better Business Bureau
4200 Wilson Boulevard, Suite 800
Arlington, VA 22203
www.give.org

The BBB Wise Giving Alliance collects and distributes information on hundreds of nonprofit organizations that solicit nationally or have national or international program services. The Web site is one of the best resources for evaluating nonprofits in this country. Visit www.give.org/reports to get detailed charity reports for hundreds of nonprofits. You will find information about an organization's history, its finances, the CEO or executive salaries, staff and board membership, and fund-raising efficiency.

Guidestar
427 Scotland Street
Williamsburg, VA 23185
757-229-4631 phone
www.guidestar.org

Guidestar is a national database of nonprofit organizations around the country. It gathers and distributes data on more than 850,000 IRS-recognized nonprofits. Visit the Guidestar Web site for comprehensive financial and statistical information on your favorite nonprofit.

Independent Sector
1200 18th Street NW, Suite 200
Washington, DC 20036
202-467-6100 phone
202-467-6101 fax
www.independentsector.org

The Independent Sector is a coalition of leading nonprofits, foundations, and corporations intended to strengthen not-for-profit initiatives, philanthropy, and citizen action. Its Web site has valuable resources for the nonprofit insider as well as the donor or volunteer.

BoardSource
1828 L Street NW, Suite 900
Washington, DC 20036
800-883-6262 phone
202-452-6299 fax
www.ncnb.org

BoardSource is a premier resource for practical information, tools and best practices, training, and leadership development for board members of nonprofit organizations worldwide.

Chronicle of Philanthropy
1255 23rd St. NW, Suite 700
Washington, DC 20037
202-466-1200 phone
www.philanthropy.com

The *Chronicle of Philanthropy* is a biweekly newspaper of the nonprofit world. It is the one of the leading resources of news and events for charity leaders, fund-raisers, grant makers, and other people involved in the philanthropic enterprise. The Web site has an excellent job board and reference section (for subscribers only).

Charity Navigator
1200 MacArthur Boulevard
Mahwah, New Jersey 07430
201-818-1288 phone
201-818-4694 fax
www.charitynavigator.org

Charity Navigator tracks the financial performance of 2,500 charities around the country. Using data from tax reports, it calculates the efficacy of a nonprofit's giving and spending habits by measuring them against seven benchmarks. Each nonprofit is assigned a rating from one to four stars, similar to Morningstar's mutual-fund rating system.

Kitchens in National Cooperation: Registered Kitchens and Other Partners

Please support or visit a local program in your area

Amos House	415 Friendship Street	Providence	RI	02907	401-831-9866	www.amoshouse.com
Back to Basics—Arcata Endeavor	501 9th Street	Arcata	CA	95521	707-822-5008	www.northoast.com/~endeavor
Bread and Butter Cafe Community	719 E. Broad Street	Savannah	GA	31415	912-236-6750	www.helpendhunger.org
California Emergency Foodlink	5 Foodlink Street	Sacramento	CA	95828	916-387-9000	www.foodlink.org
Campus Kitchens Project	6979 Dartmouth Avenue	St. Louis	MO	63130	314-725-8475	www.campuskitchens.org
Central Wyoming Community Kitchen	PO Box 3212	Casper	WY	82602	307-265-2251	cwrm@cwrm.org
CFLS Restaurant	500 3rd Street NW	Washington	DC	20001	202-347-7035	
Channels Food Rescue	PO Box 724	New Cumberland	PA	17070	717-612-1300	www.paonline.com/channels
Chicago's Community Kitchen	1116 N. Kedzie Avenue	Chicago	IL	60651	773-772-7170	
Cincinnati COOKS!	425 Ezzard Charles Drive	Cincinnati	OH	45203	513-929-0904	

continued on next page

Organization	Address	City	State	Zip	Phone	Website
City Harvest	575 8th Avenue	New York	NY	10018	917-351-8700	www.cityharvest.org
Clara White Mission	613 West Ashley Street	Jacksonville	FL	32202	904-354-4162	www.clarawhitemission.org
Cleveland Community Kitchen	11770 Berea Road	Cleveland	OH	44111	216-688-1212	www.clevelandfoodbank.com
Community Culinary School of Charlotte	2410-A Distribution Street	Charlotte	NC	28203	704-375-4500	
Community Food Bank of New Jersey	31 Evans Terminal Road	Hillside	NJ	07205-2400	908-335-3663	njfoodbank.org
Community Kitchen of Hope	595 Ragsdale Street	Jacksonville	TX	75766	903-586-7781	wakemow.home.mindspring.com/foodrun.html
Community Kitchen of Monroe County, Inc.	917 S. Rogers Street	Bloomington	IN	47403	812-332-0999	www.bloomington.in.us/socserv/iris/Community_Kitchen.html
Conquering Homelessness Through Employment in Food	705 Natoma Street	San Francisco	CA	94103	415-487-3790	ecs-sf.org
County of Ventura	Senior Nutrition Program	Camarillo	CA	93010	805-987-2454	
Cuyahoga County Workforce Development	1275 Ontario Street	Cleveland	OH	44113	216-698-2887	
Daily Bread	PO Box 6042	Leesburg	VA	20175	703-777-5911	www.interfaithrelief.org
Damiano Center	206 W. 4th Street	Duluth	MN	55806	218-772-8708	www.damianocenter.org

D.C. Central Kitchen	425 2nd Street NW	Washington	DC	20001	202-234-0707	www.dccentralkitchen.org
East End Kid's Katering	215 Congress Street	Portland	ME	04103	207-871-8810	
Elijah's Promise	18 Neilson Street	New Brunswick	NJ	08901	732-545-9002	www.elijahspromise.org
Family Affair Ministries Community Kitchen@Berkshi	1500 Porter Road	Nashville	TN	37216	615-228-0125	faminc.org
FareStart	1902 2nd Avenue	Seattle	WA	98109	206-443-1233	www.farestart.org
Food Bank of Delaware's Community Kitchen	Delaware Industrial Park 14 Garland Way	Newark	DE	19713	302-292-1305	www.fbd.org
Food Bank of Monmouth and Ocean Counties	3300 Route 55	Neptune	NJ	07753	732-918-2600	www.foodbankmoc.org
Food Gatherers	1731 Dhu Varren Road	Ann Arbor	MI	48105	734-761-2796	
Food Share	4156 N. Southbank Road	Oxnard	CA	93036	805-983-7100	foodshare.com
Foodlink	936 Exchange Street	Rochester	NY	14608	585-328-3380	www.foodlinkny.org
Haight Ashbury Food Program	1525 Waller Street	San Francisco	CA	94117	415-503-4480	www.thefoodprogram.org
Harvest Texarkana	PO Box 707	Texarkana	TX	75504	903-794-1398	

continued on next page

APPENDIX

201

Name	Address	City	State	ZIP	Phone	Website
Inspiration Cafe	4554 N. Broadway, Suite 207	Chicago	IL	60601	773-878-0981	www.inspirationcafe.org
Inter-faith Food Shuttle	216 Lord Anson Drive	Raleigh	NC	27610	919-250-0043	www.foodshuttle.org
KCCK Culinary Cornerstones	PO Box 410616	Kansas City	MO	64141	816-474-6524	
Kitchen of Opportunities	3025 4th Avenue South	Minneapolis	MN	55408	612-827-2085	www.2harvest.org
Kitchens in National Cooperation	1302 Walthour Road	Savannah	GA	31410	912-898-0595	www.kitchensinc.org
Louisville Community Kitchen	PO Box 35458	Louisville	KY	40232	502-966-3821	daretocare.org
Meet Each Need with Dignity (MEND)	13460 Van Nuys Boulevard	Pacoima	CA	91331	818-896-0246	www.mendpoverty.org
Memphis Community Kitchen	239 South Dudley	Memphis	TN	38104	901-323-6226	www.memphisfoodbank.org
Movable Feast	PO Box 2298	Baltimore	MD	21203-2298	410-327-3420	www.mfeast.org
My Brother's Keeper II	PO Box 374	Abbeville	SC	29620	864-391-2418	
New Day Community Kitchen	3320 E. Van Buren	Phoenix	AZ	85008	602-275-7852	www.umom.org
North Texas Food Bank	4306 Shilling Way	Dallas	TX	75237	214-330-1396	ntfb.org

Philabundance Community Kitchen	3149 Germantown Avenue	Philadelphia	PA	19133	215-221-1700	www.philabundance.org
Project Host, Soup Kitchen	PO Box 345	Greenville	SC	29602	864-235-3403	www.projecthost.org
Rachel's Table Community Kitchen at Life Haven	360 Amity Road	Woodbridge	CT	06525	203-387-2424	www.rachelstable.com
Rhode Island Community Kitchen	104 Hay Street	West Warwick	RI	02893	401-826-3073	www.rifoodbank.org
St. Louis University Campus Kitchen	3753 West Pine Mall	St. Louis	MO	63101	314-977-3881	www.campuskitchens.org
Samosaman Natural Foods	PO Box 1029	Barre	VT	05641	802-233-7783	
School as Community Kitchen	7042 W. Fagler Street	Miami	FL	33144	786-275-0446	
Second Harvest Food Bank of the Chattahoochee Valley	5928 Coca-Cola Boulevard	Columbus	GA	31909	706-561-4755	
Second Helpings	3324 E. Michigan Street, Suite 150	Indianapolis	IN	46201	317-632-2664	www.secondhelpings.org
Senior Nutrition Program	PO Box 51650	Knoxville	TN	37950	865-524-2786	www.kormet.org/ooa/meals.htm
South Plains Food Bank	4612 Locust Avenue	Lubbock	TX	79404	806-763-3003	
St. Francis House	39 Boylston Street	Boston	MA	02112	617-542-4211	www.stfrancishouse.org

continued on next page

St. Luke's United Methodist Church	3655 Calvert Street NW	Washington	DC	20007	202-333-4949	www.saintlukesmethodist.org
St. Mary's Food Bank	1818 E. 16th Street	Phoenix	AZ	85034	602-322-0161	www.smfb.org
Sutherland Culinary Services	208 S. LaSalle, Suite 1818	Chicago	IL	60604	312-660-1381	www.heartland-alliance.org
Tarrant Area Food Bank	2600 Cullen Street	Fort Worth	TX	76107	817-332-9177	www.tafb.org
Technical College of the Low Country	PO Box 1288	Beaufort	SC	29901-1288	843-470-8385	tcl.edu
Temple Brotherhood Mission	PO Box 29245	Philadelphia	PA	19125	215-739-4495	
Texas Christian University	Texas Christian University	Fort Worth	TX	76129	817-257-6321	tcu.edu
The Atlanta Collaborative Kitchen (TACK)	176 Ottley Drive, NE	Atlanta	GA	30324	404-419-3336	ProjectOpenHand.org
The Community Kitchen Inc.	PO Box 1315	Keene	NH	03431	603-352-3200	www.thecommunitykitchen.org
The Memphis TN Food Bank	239 S. Dudley	Memphis	TN	38104	901-405-0071	www.memphisfoodbank.org
Trenton Area Soup Kitchen	PO Box 872	Trenton	NJ	08605	609-695-5456	www.trentonsoupkitchen.org
Triad Community Kitchen	3210 Clamoor Drive	Winston-Salem	NC	27127	336-399-6774	

Urban Horizons Food Company	50 E. 168th Street	The Bronx	NY	10452	718-839-1100	www.whedco.org
Vermont Foodbank	PO Box 254	South Barre	VT	05670	802-476-3341	
Wallace Academy Community Kitchen	1101 6th Avenue	Nashville	TN	37208	615-460-4430	www.centerstone.org
Wayside Evening Soup Kitchen	PO Box 1278	Portland	ME	04104	207-775-4939	www.waysidesoupkitchen.org
Weems Academy Community Kitchen	252 Oxford Street	Clarksville	TN	37040	931-920-7382	centerstone.org
Westside Food Bank	PO Box 1310	Sun City	AZ	85372	623-344-2157	www.westsidefoodbank.org
Women's Community Building Kitchen	100 W. Seneca Street	Ithaca	NY	14850	607-272-1247	www.lightlink.com/womens
Worcester County Food Bank	474 Boston Turnpike (Rt. 9)	Shrewsbury	MA	01545	508-842-3663	www.foodbank.org

INDEX

A2H. *See* America's Second Harvest
AA. *See* Alcoholics Anonymous
Abel Foundation, 35
abolitionist movement, 173–74, 179
Ad Council, 122–23
administrative overhead, 16–17
  in community kitchens, 164
  in nonprofits, 79–80, 147, 180,
    182
  at United Way of D.C., 147
advertising, 16
advocacy, 37–38
  for nonprofit sector, 47
  for social reform, 161–63
African AIDSTrek, 92
African American history month,
    D.C. Central Kitchen event for,
    118
Age of Enlightenment, 4

Agricultural Adjustment
    Administration, 10
Agriculture Department, U.S., 82,
    105–6, 159
AIDS/HIV, 156
  Greyston Foundation treatment,
    137
AIDS kitchens, 164
AIDSRide bicycle trips, 92, 93
Albuquerque (N.M.) Campus
    Kitchen Project, 106
Alcoholics Anonymous, 42
Allen, Steve, 146
allocation
  of taxes, 167
  of United Way of D.C. donations,
    171
Altria, 164
American Express, 90, 91

American Red Cross, xx, 7, 20
  designated donations and, 79, 80
American School Food Service
  Association (ASFSA), 106
America's Promise, 139–40
America's Second Harvest (A2H),
  20, 44, 82
  public service announcements for,
  122–24, 125–26
AmeriCorps, 17, 151
Anthony, Susan B., 173
AOL, 107–8
Aramony, William, 147–49
ASFSA. *See* American School Food
  Service Association
Atlanta (Ga.) United Way, 171
Augsburg College Campus Kitchen
  Project, 106
Avon 3-Day Walks for Breast
  Cancer, 92, 93

baby boomers, 160–61, 180
Bad Brains (music group), 26
Bandelier National Park wildfire,
  70–71
Bayou (Georgetown club), 141
BBB Wise Giving Alliance, 195–96
Beatles (music group), 174
Ben & Jerry's (company), 137,
  161–62
Better Business Bureau, 97
  BBB Wise Giving Alliance,
  195–96
big business
  philanthropy as, 11–15
  See also corporations
big government, 11
Bill and Melinda Gates Foundation,
  20
Blame Society stereotype, 67–68
Blame the Victim stereotype, 67, 68
board oversight, of nonprofit sector,
  150, 163
BoardSource, 197
Boeing (company), 101

Borchert, Karen, 105–6
Bowie, David, 142
"Brand New Day" (song), 111
Bread for the World, 82
breast cancer movement, 90–91, 93
Breedlove (Lubbock, Tex.), 158
Bridges, Beau and Jeff, xvi
Brookings Institution, 96
Buffett, Warren, 49
Burger King, 140
Burns, Mike, 101–2
bus desegregation, 74–75
Bush, George H. W., xvi, 23, 36, 37,
  112, 156
businesses. *See* corporations; for-
  profit companies; nonprofit
  sector
business incubator, nonprofit,
  83–84
Byrd, Charlie, 27

calculated epiphany, 110, 125–31
California, 72–74
Campus Kitchen Project, 104–6
Canty, Brendan, 180
capital campaigns, 49–53, 102
Carnegie, Andrew, 12, 13, 14, 71,
  181
  philanthropy concept of, 3–7, 8,
  18, 164–65
Carnegie Endowment for
  International Peace, 8
Carnegie Foundation, 20
Carnegie Foundation for the
  Advancement of Teaching, 6
Carnegie Hall, 6
Carnegie libraries, 7
Carnegie Mellon University, 6
Carnegie Steel, 6
Casablanca (film), 25–26
Cash, Johnny, 60
caste system, client, 123, 179
Catholic Church, 3
cause, as priority of doing good, 88,
  178

cause-based marketing, 16, 90–93,
    162–63
CEO (nonprofits) compensation,
    189–94
certified food handler test, 41–42
"Changes" (song), 142
"Changing of the Guards" (song),
    143
charity
    community building vs., 161–62
    demographics of contributions to,
        45–46
    nonprofit budget commitment to,
        16–17
    philanthropy differentiated from,
        4, 5
    "soup kitchen" stereotype of, xvi,
        xvii
    tax-deductible contributions to,
        11
    U.S. giving statistics (2000), 186
    See also philanthropy
Charity, Philanthropy and Civility
    in American History
    (Sealander), 8–9
Charity Navigator, 198
Charlie's (jazz club), 27–28, 32,
    138, 144–47
Chavez, Caesar, 183
child care center, 137, 140
Childe Harold (blues club), 26
Chronicle of Philanthropy
    (newspaper), 197
Churchill, Winston, 80
Cinco de Mayo, D.C. Central
    Kitchen event for, 118
City Harvest, 33
civic societies, 4
Civilian Conservation Corps, 10
Civil Rights movement, 74–75, 76,
    183
Civil Works Administration, 10
Clash (music group), xx
client
    caste system, 123, 179

as priority of doing good, 88–89,
    178
Clinton, Bill, xvi, 151, 159
Clinton, Hillary Rodham, xvi, 151
Clooney, Rosemary, 27, 145
Coltrane, John, 181
community, as priority, 89–90, 178
community building, 161–62,
    180–81
Community Chest, 8, 9–10, 12
community kitchens, xvi, 108, 164
    school-based cafeterias as, 104–6
complacency, nonprofits and,
    143–54, 157, 163
consolidation, agency, 163–64
Cool Hand Luke (film), 121
Cornell School of Hotel
    Administration, 41
Cornell University, 173
corporations
    cause-based marketing by, 90–93
    entrepreneurial vision and,
        133–36
    federal nonprofit donations policy
        for, 159
    philanthropy rules for, 180–82
    tax-exemptions and shelters for,
        10–11
    2002 contributions by, 188
crack use, 42
credibility, of nonprofits, 178

Dallas (Tex.) food bank, 158–59
D.C. Central Kitchen, xv–xvi,
    19–20, 175–76, 195
    Campus Kitchen Project and,
        104–6
    credit union of, 51
    drug testing by, 2, 42, 111
    federal funding and, 57–60, 167
    First Helping outreach program
        and, 151
    founding of, 25–47, 112
    Fresh Start for-profit catering unit
        of, 51, 60, 126–27

D.C. Central Kitchen (*cont.*)
   holiday event sponsorship by, 118–19
   job-training program of, xv, 1–2, 41–42, 51, 57–59, 89, 98, 110–15, 127
   organizational effectiveness of, 98–100, 102
   salaries, 149
   Summer Food program, 151
   tangible link and, 112–15, 117–19
   volunteer issues, 64, 68, 85–88, 113–15, 128–29
deer hunting, 159
dehydrated food, 158
Delancy Street (San Francisco social enterprise), 90
Dell, Michael, 136
designated donations, 79–80, 171
Dignity Project (Gainesville, Fla., car repair organization), 116–17, 119
Dillard University Campus Kitchen Project, 106
District of Columbia, xv–viii, xxi, 18, 41–42, 130. *See also* D.C. Central Kitchen
Dodge brothers, 124, 140, 142
donations. *See* charity; individual donors; philanthropy
Donna, Roberto, 41
Douglass, Frederick, 173
drug testing, 2, 42, 111
drug-treatment programs, 130
drug use, xv, 42, 156
Dukakis, Michael, 36
Dylan, Bob, 143

Eagle, Bryan, 83–84
Eastern State Penitentiary, 5
Eckstine, Billy, 27
Edmund Burke Middle School (D.C.), 118
Emerge Memphis, 84

employment policies. *See* jobs; job training
empowerment programs, 83–84
entrepreneurial vision, 133–38
epiphany, calculated, 110, 125–31
Eureka vacuum cleaners, 90, 91
Ewing, J. R. (fictional character), 90

fair wages, stereotypes of, 65–66
FareStart (Seattle training kitchen), 89
Federal City Shelter, 43–44
Federal Deposit Insurance Corporation, 10
federal funding of nonprofits, 12–13, 57–60
Federal Tax Act of 1935, 10
Financial Times (London), xvi
First Helping (outreach program), 151
Fish Market (cabaret), 26
Fitzgerald, Ella, 144
501(c)(3) tax status, 11–12, 13
flash frozen food, 159
Folger Shakespeare Library (D.C.), 119
food, 81–83, 157–60
   Campus Kitchen Project, 104–6
   community kitchens, 104, 108, 164
   Grate Patrol volunteer program, 28–32, 33–34, 37, 83, 96, 174–75
   Kitchens, Inc., 44, 164, 195, 199–205
   war on hunger and, 19–20, 63–68, 111, 156–62
   See also D.C. Central Kitchen; hunger
food banks, 108, 122, 156
   North Texas, 158–59
Foodchain, 44
Food Donor and Donee Act of 1998, 159
food industry, 157–58

food pantries, 81–83
Food Research and Action Center
  (FRAC), 82
Ford, Edsel, 11
Ford, Henry, 11, 40, 139, 142, 165
  vision of, 133–34, 135, 136
Ford Foundation, 10–11, 20
for-profit companies
  cause-based marketing by, 90–93
  Fresh Start, 51, 126–27
  See also corporations
foster care, 72–74
foundations
  philanthropy rules for, 180–82
  tax incentives for, 10–11
  2002 contributions by, 188
  2002 contributions to, 187
48 Hours (television program), xvi
FRAC. *See* Food Research and
  Action Center
Franklin, Benjamin, 4, 13, 115
Fresh Start, 51, 126–27
friendship, meaning of, 174–75
Fugazi (music group), 180
fund-raising efficiency, 16–17

Gainesville, Fla., 116–17, 119
Gandhi, Mahatma, 74, 75–76, 166,
  183
Gardner, John, 155, 177
Gates, Bill, 20, 136
Gates, Frederick, 7
Gates Foundation, 20
gender, nonprofit compensation by,
  192–94
General Mills, 156
Georgetown Day School, 87
Georgetown University, 41
Getz, Stan, 27
Giant Steps (Coltrane), 181
Gilberto, Astrud, 27, 145–46
"Giving in America" (Gross), 4
Glassman, Bernard, 136–38, 139,
  142
Glickman, Dan, 159

Globe Theater cake replica, 119
Gochnauer, Dick, 73
"good intentions gone bad," 53
Goodwill Industries, 7
"Gospel of Wealth, The"
  (Carnegie), 18
government, 9–10, 15, 167, 181
  nonprofit funding by, 12–13,
  57–60
  *See also specific agencies and
  programs*
Grace Church (D.C.), 28–29, 31
Grate Patrol (volunteer food
  program), 28–34, 37, 83, 96,
  174–75
Great Depression (1930s), 9–11
Great Society, 12–14
Greyston Bakery (Yonkers, N.Y.),
  136–38
Greyston Foundation, 137
Gross, Robert, 4
Guest, Christopher, 138
Guidestar (online nonprofits
  resource), 149, 196
  2002 compensation report,
  188–94

Habitat for Humanity, 98–99, 105,
  167
  tangible link and, 115–16, 119
Habro, 101
Hammurabi, king of Babylonia, 4
Harris, Emmylou, 26
Harvard University, 66
Hicks, Beecher, 95
high school volunteers, 103–4
Hirt, Al, 27
HIV. *See* AIDS/HIV
Holiday, Billie, 144
homelessness, xv, xvi, 2, 156, 179
  Grate Patrol volunteer food
  program, 28–34, 37, 83, 96,
  174–75
Hoop Dreams (D.C. scholarship
  program), 172

housing, 18, 179
  for foster children, 72–74
  Greyston Foundation and, 137
  See also homelessness
Housing and Urban Development
    (HUD) Department, U.S., 57,
    59
hunger, 1, 2, 37–38, 55–56, 179
  obesity and, 159–60, 161
  stereotyping and, xvi, 63–64,
    111
  See also food; War on Hunger

Iggy Pop, 141–42
"Imagine" (song), 169
"I'm Bored" (song), 142
impact agenda, 171
income tax. *See* taxes
Independent Sector (nonprofit
    coalition), 196–97
India, 74, 75–76, 166, 183
individual donors
  rules for, 182–84
  2000 contributions by, 186
  See also charity
industrial empires, 133–36
inner city nonprofits, 163
Invisible Hand (Smith economic
    concept), 21

Jerk, The (film), 35
Job Corps, 12
jobs
  Greyston Foundation and, 137
  nonprofit compensation by
    category, 192–93
  stereotyping of, 65–66
  wages and, 65–66, 133–34
job training
  by D.C. Central Kitchen, xv, 1–2,
    41–42, 51, 57–59, 89, 98,
    109–15, 127
  federal legislation, 15
Johnson, Lyndon B., 12–14, 18,
    123

Kay, Susie, 172
Kellogg Foundation, 20
Kellogg's (company), 156
Kennedy, John F., 12, 13, 15, 123
Kennedy, Robert, 184
KFC (company), 159
King, Martin Luther, Jr., 74–75, 76,
    112, 166, 183
Kingston Trio (music group), 27
Kitchen Aid mixers, 90, 91
Kitchens, INC (Kitchens in National
    Cooperation), 44, 164, 195,
    199–205
Klc, Steve, 118–19
Kraft Foods, 156
Kroc, Ray, 134–36, 140, 142
Krupin, Mel, 118

Labor Department, U.S., 57, 58, 59
law of unintended consequences, 53
Lawrence (Mass.) Campus Kitchen
    Project, 106
leadership, 182
leadership programs, 153–54
Lennon, John, 169
libraries, 4, 7
literacy, 42
Livingston, Todd, 116–17
living wage, 107–8
local government, 181
Loyola College Campus Kitchen
    Project, 106
Lubbock, Texas, 158
Luke, Gospel According to, 76–77

Manpower Development and
    Training Act, 15
March of Dimes, 71–72, 74, 75
Mariners' Church (Irvine, Calif.), 72
Marquette University Campus
    Kitchen Project, 106
Marriott (company), 159
Martin, Steve, 35
McCartney, Paul, 174
McDonald, Dick and Maurice, 135

McDonald's (company), 135–36, 139–40, 142

McRae, Carmen, 145

Meals on Wheels, 105–6, 108, 160–61, 164

Medicaid and Medicare, 13

Memphis (Tenn.) business incubator, 83–84

Mezza Café (Starbucks), 101

Miami (Fla.) Campus Kitchen Project, 106

Model T (Ford car), 133, 134

Montgomery (Ala.) bus boycott, 74–75, 183

Mother's March Campaign (March of Dimes), 71–72

Multimixer (blender), 134, 135

My Man Godfrey (film), 109

Narcotics Anonymous, 42

National Labor Relations Board, 10

National Recovery Administration, 10

National Restaurant Association, 139

Neighborhood Youth Program, 12

New Deal, 10–11, 18

Newman, Paul, xvi, 161

Newman's Own (company), 161

New York Times (newspaper), xvi

Nightline (television program), xvi

Nirvana (rock band), 177

nonprofit sector, xv–xvii
  administrative overhead, 79–80, 147, 180, 182
  advocacy model for, 47
  agency consolidation, 163–64
  beginnings of, 3–7
  board oversight of, 150, 163
  business incubator, 83–84
  as career path, 2
  categories and growth of, xvii
  compensation. *See subhead* salaries *below*

complacency and, 143–54, 157, 163
  creative destruction and, 22
  credibility of, 178
  efficiency and, 16–17, 96–97, 102, 163, 178, 180
  future of, 159–68
  growth of, 9–15
  inner city, 163
  innovation and, 138–42
  leadership programs for, 153–54
  management model for, 47
  organizational effectiveness of, 96–97
  oversight of, 150, 163, 178
  propaganda for, 15–16, 123
  resource competition by, 7–8, 44–46, 52, 78–79, 182
  revenues of, 20–21, 59–60
  rules for, 177–84
  salaries, 17, 44, 54–55, 98–99, 188–94
  stereotyping in, 1, 64–65, 111
  suburban, 163
  tax laws and, 10–11

North Texas Food Bank (Dallas), 158–59

Northwestern University Campus Kitchen Project, 106

nutritional imperialists, 85–86

nutritional value, 159–60

obesity, 159–60, 161

Odysseus, 124, 131

Oldfield, Mike, 26

Orange County (Calif.) foster care, 72–74

Orangewood Children's Foundation, 72

organizational effectiveness, 96

oversight, nonprofit, 150, 163, 178

Palladin, Jean-Louis, 41

Pallotta, Dan, 92

Pallotta TeamWorks, 92–93

parable of widow's mite (Luke),
  76–77
Parks, Rosa, 74
Passover, D.C. Central Kitchen
  event for, 118
Patton, George, 19, 136
Peace Corps, 17, 151
Peterson, Oscar, 146
Philadelphia, Pa., 5–6
philanthropy, 180–84
  as big business, 11–15
  Carnegie and Rockefeller
    philosophy of, 3–7, 8, 18,
    164–65
  charity vs., 4, 5
  by corporations and foundations,
    180–82
  designated donations and, 79–80,
    171
  donor constituents and, 89–90,
    178
  Franklin concept of, 5–6, 115
  by individual donors (2000),
    186
  results-oriented, 161–62
  rules for individual donors,
    182–84
  types of recipient organizations
    (2002), 187
Pioneer Human Services, 101–2,
  108, 162
Pizza Hut, 159
Porter, Cole, 146
Poullion, Nora, 41
poverty, 3, 6, 18, 179. *See also* War
  on Hunger; War on Poverty
Powell, Colin, 139
priorities, 88–90
prison reform, 5
professional services, 163
profit and purpose, 166–67, 183
  industrial empires and, 133–36
  social change and, 166–67
protein, 159
public libraries, 4, 7

public service announcements, 16,
  122–24, 125–26
public works, 10
purpose. *See* profit and purpose

race-based policies, 13
Ramon, Jose, 41
Ramones (music group), 26
Reagan, Ronald, 11
Red Cross. *See* American Red Cross
relief programs, 10
Republic Tea, 90
resource competition
  donor constituent guidelines and,
    89–90
  by nonprofits, xvii, 7–8, 44–46,
    52, 78–79, 182
Rising Tide (nonprofit program),
  72–74, 76, 167
Rockefeller, John D., 12, 13, 71,
  164–65, 181
  philanthropy concept of, 3–5, 74
Rockefeller Foundation, 20
Rockefeller Institute for Medical
  Research, 7
Roosevelt, Franklin D.
  March of Dimes and, 71
  New Deal and, 10, 11, 18
Rosenwald, Julius, 6
rules for nonprofit sector, 177–84
Rush, Benjamin, 4, 5

Safe Haven (drug-treatment
  program), 130
Sage, Olivia, 6
Sahl, Mort, 146
St. Louis (Mo.) Campus Kitchen
  Project, 104–6
St. Patrick's Day, D.C. Central
  Kitchen event for, 118
salaries
  living wage and, 107–8
  in nonprofit sector, 17, 44, 54–55,
    98–99, 149–50, 178, 182–83,
    188–94

at United Way of America, 54, 55, 146

Sales Brothers (rock band), 141–42

Salk, Jonas, 72

Salt Act protest march (India), 75–76, 183

Salvation Army, 7, 9, 20, 29, 65, 96, 105

San Francisco, Calif., 90

SAS (software company), 165–66

SAT scores, 18

Savannah (Ga.) Campus Kitchen Project, 106

school-based cafeterias, 103–6

Sealander, Judith, 8–9

Sears Roebuck (company), 6

Seattle, Wash., 89

Securities and Exchange Commission, 10

"Send in the Clowns" (song), 154

Shakespeare, William, birthday celebration for, 119

Shaw Pittman (law firm), 106

Short, Bobby, 27, 146

Silbert, Mimi, 90

Sixteenth Amendment, 11

Sixth Sense, The (film), 170

skepticism, 177

Sly and the Family Stone (music group), 20

Smith, Adam, 21

Smithsonian Institution, 39

social change, 16, 166–68, 170–71
  activist agents for, 74–76, 166–67, 183
  advocates for, 161–63
  government and, 167
  issue politicization and, 13
  profit and purpose as formula for, 166–67

social Darwinism, 3

Social Gospel, 3, 11

social reform. *See* social change

social responsibility, 161–62

Social Security Administration, 10

social strategy, random acts of kindness vs., 69–80, 183

Sodexho, 104, 159

Sondheim, Stephen, 154

"soup kitchen" stereotype, xv–xviii, 128

Sowell, Thomas, 149

Standard Oil (company), 7, 165

Starbucks (company), 101

Starr, Ringo, 173

stereotyping, xv–xviii, 63–68, 111, 128
  volunteers and, 64, 68, 113–15
  war on hunger and, 63–64

Strummer, Joe, xx

suburban nonprofits, 163

Summer Food program at D.C. Central Kitchen, 151

Supreme Court, U.S., 75

Syracuse University, 173

tangible link, 110–19, 178

Target (company), 165

taxes, 10–13
  allocation of, 167
  exemption and deduction incentives, 10–12, 13, 157

tax shelters, 10–11

Teach for America, 17

Tennessee Valley Authority, 10

Texas
  Breedlove nonprofit, 158
  Dallas food bank, 158–59

This Is Spinal Tap (film), 138

Thompson, Hunter S., 180

Thousand Points of Light (G.H.W. Bush concept), xvi, 23, 36

Thurgood Marshall Building (D.C.), 129

Timberland (company), 165

Today (television show), xvi

Todd, Chapman, 40, 45

Tormé, Mel, 27, 138

Trojan horse, 124–25, 131

Truth, Sojourner, 173
Tubman, Harriet, 172–74, 179

Underground Railroad, 173, 179
unemployment, 9
unintended consequences, law of, 53
Union Station (D.C.), 129
United Way of America, xx, 8, 20, 139, 181, 183
    Aramony and, 147–49
    impact agenda of, 171
United Way of Atlanta, 171
United Way of D.C., xviii, 53–55, 146, 170–72
    CEO stereotyping at, 64–65
    giving strategies and, 78–80
United Way of the National Capital Area. *See* United Way of D.C.
Universal Life Church, 43
University of Chicago, 7
UPS (company), 38
USDA. *See* Agriculture Department, U.S.

Vaughan, Sarah, 27, 144–47, 154
venison, 159
volunteers
    demographics of, 45–46
    foster care housing and, 73
    hours given by, xviii, 181
    personal agendas of, 86–87
    preconceived ideas of, 85–88
    professional services performed by, 163
    rules for, 182–84
    stereotyping by, 64, 68, 113–15, 128–29
    2000 statistics on, 186
    youths as, 78, 87, 103–6, 151–53, 178

Wacoal bra fitting, 90
wages, 107–8, 133–34
    stereotypes of fair, 65–66
    See also salaries
Wall Street Journal (newspaper), xvi
War on Hunger, 19–20, 46, 81–83, 122–23
    future of, 156–62
    stereotyping and, 63–68, 111
War on Poverty, 12, 15–16, 18
Washington, D.C. *See* District of Columbia
Washington Post (newspaper), xvi, 37, 55, 56
Watson, Lila, 81
web sites, 195–98
Westchester County, N.Y., 136–38
Westerberg, Paul, 1
West Point, N.Y., 136
Winfrey, Oprah, xvi
"With a Little Help from My Friends" (song), 174
Withers, Bill, 111
Wizard of Oz (film), 69
women's suffrage movement, 173
work associations, 4
Works Progress Administration, 10
work-study programs, 12
World Court Building (The Hague), 6–7
World Health Organization, 160
World War I, 8
World War II, 11

Yaffe, Ian, 87, 106
YMCA, 7
Yonkers, N.Y., 136–38
youth volunteers, 78, 87, 103–6, 151–53, 178
YWCA, 7

Zaytinya (restaurant), 119

ABOUT THE AUTHORS

ROBERT EGGER is the president and founder of the D.C. Central Kitchen in Washington, D.C. He travels extensively promoting nonprofit innovation to everyone from Fortune 500 companies and business schools to college campuses and culinary institutes. The Kitchen was named one of the President Bush Sr.'s Thousand Points of Light, and has been featured on *Oprah, Nightline,* and *48 Hours* as well as in the *Washington Post,* the *Financial Times,* the *Wall Street Journal,* and numerous other publications. In 2002, he volunteered to serve as interim director of the United Way National Capital Area to reorganize its struggling executive leadership. He is the recipient of the Oprah "Angel" award, the Bender Prize, and a Caring Award. He lives in Washington, D.C.

HOWARD YOON is a writer, editor, and literary agent based in Washington, D.C. He has collaborated with authors on numerous nonfiction book projects. He lives in Arlington, Virginia.